SWITZERLAND

△ **Geneva (p30)**
Home to international organisations from the UN to the Red Cross, Geneva is also the birthplace of Rousseau and Voltaire.

▷ **Zillis (p61)**
The Martinskirche here has an extraordinary painted wooded ceiling of 153 panels, dating from around 1160.

▽ **St Gallen (p58)** As well as being one of Europe's most important spiritual centres, this monastery houses a superb rococo library with many rare texts.

△ **Rhine Falls (p47)**
These thunderous falls on the Rhine are an awe-inspiring sight.

◁ **Lake Lugano (p56)**
The lake's Mediterranean climate and Alpine views are a lovely combination

△ **Zürich (p39)**
Switzerland's largest city and its financial centre. The banks are legendary, as is the shopping along Bahnhofstrasse.

△ **Eiger, Mönch and Jungfrau (p92)** The classic trio of Swiss mountains; the Eiger's north face is infamous, while the Jungfraujoch offers breathtaking views.

▽ **Matterhorn (p97)**
This spectacular and unmistakeable Alpine peak has seen many mountaineering dramas.

△ **Basel (p20)**
Cosmopolitan Basel has a long and distinguished cultural history.

◁ **Engadine (p84)**
This region has some of the country's best and most varied scenery.

An Exceptional Country

Switzerland has always been regarded as something of an exception. Despite being a relatively small country, it's a leading economic power; although it has hardly any natural resources other than water power, it's still incredibly wealthy. A country of four distinct languages, it nevertheless suffers few ethnic problems. Situated in the centre of Europe, and often surrounded by monarchs, emperors and dictators, it has stubbornly managed to maintain independence and preserve a form of democracy for 700 years. It is the European seat of the UN but only in March 2002, after much hesitation, did it vote to become a member.

Opposite: the Matterhorn Below: the Swiss flag in reflection on Zürich's Bahnhofstrasse

CONTRADICTION AND COINCIDENCE

These may appear to be contradictions at first glance, but they are not. It was the lack of raw materials that forced the Swiss to be inventive, and it was the threat – real or apparent – from powerful neighbours that forced the country to unite, regardless of its linguistic borders. The famous Swiss author Friedrich Dürrenmatt might have been right when he maintained that Switzerland, historically, is more or less a coincidence.

Foreign visitors – especially the British – long ago discovered Switzerland's most treasured possession, its landscape. This prompted the Swiss to transform the rocky massifs and icy expanses into an important branch of their economy. One hundred years ago this was a modest little state, poor, but with, for the time, an exemplary democratic system; today it is one of the world's most popular holiday destinations, not cheap but still good value, providing quality rather than quantity. The infrastructure is excellent, and the SBB trains travel with a punctuality that has become legendary.

In this country, the depth of the bank vaults equals the height of the mountains, and guests are greeted with *Grüezi – Bonjour – Buon Giorno – Allegra!*

POSITION AND SIZE

Alpine flora in Geneva's botanical gardens

Switzerland – or the Swiss Confederation, to use its official name – lies landlocked at the very heart of Europe, occupying a surface area of 41,923sq km (16,186sq miles). It extends between latitudes 45°49' and 47°49' north and longitudes 5°57' and 10°30' east. It is bordered by Austria, the principality of Liechtenstein, Italy, France and Germany. Its frontier is almost 1,900km (1,180 miles) long. Nearly two-thirds of Switzerland is taken up by the Alps, which run across the country from southwest to northeast; to the northwest of the Alps, the much lower Jura covers around a sixth of the country; and the densely-populated Mittelland lies between these two mountain ranges, extending all the way from Lac Léman (Lake Geneva) to the Bodensee (Lake Constance).

MOUNTAINS

The longitudinal valley formed by the Rhône and the Upper Rhine divides the Alps into two main mountain ranges. The northern range can be subdivided into several major groups. To the west of the Rhône are the Savoy Alps (Dents du Midi, 3,257m/10,685ft); they are followed by the lengthy Bernese Alps, which to the west are composed mainly of limestone (Les Diablerets, 3,210m/10,531ft), and to the east of granite and gneiss. The Aare Massif, with its many glaciers, is the highest part of the Northern Alps (Finsteraarhorn, 4,272m/14,016ft; Aletschhorn, 4,195m/13,763ft; Jungfrau, 4,158m/13,641ft). To the east of the Hasli Valley are the Luzern Alps (Dammastock, 3,630m/11,909ft) which connect beyond the Reuss Valley with the Glarus Alps (Tödi, 3,614m/11,857ft).

The southern range starts in the west with the Valais Alps and reaches even higher elevations. The tallest peaks are here (Dufourspitze, 4,634m/15,203ft; Monte Rosa, 4,634m/15,203ft; Dom, 4,545m/14,911ft; Matterhorn, 4,478m/14,691ft; Dent Blanche, 4,357m/14,295ft). The deep Val Antigório separates Valais from the Ticino Alps (Basódino, 3,273m/10,738ft), which are connected in the east to the Adula Group (Rheinwaldhorn, 3,402m/11,161ft). Finally, in the Rhaetian Alps, the southern range becomes a lot broader, and high peaks appear once more in the Bernina Massif (Piz Bernina, 4,049m/13,284ft).

In the regions above 2,500m (8,200ft) the Alps contain numerous glaciers, although several of these have receded over the past few hundred years. The most impressive glaciers are in the Bernese and Valais Alps, especially the Aletsch Glacier *(see page 98)*, the largest in Europe.

The Swiss Mittelland, which gradually rises towards the Alps, is bordered to the northwest by the Jura. These lower, more gentle summits extend northeastwards from the Rhône – part of a 200-km (124-mile) long massif that slowly drops down towards the Rhine. The highest elevations are Mont Tendre (1,679m/5,500ft), Dôle (1,677m/5,500ft), Chasseral (1,607m/5,270ft) and Chasseron (1,606m/5,260ft).

RIVERS AND LAKES

All the main rivers in Switzerland have their sources in the Gotthard Massif – with the exception of the Inn, which originates in the Upper Engadine. The rivers Aare, Reuss and Rhine join up at Brugg and Waldshut and flow into the North Sea. To the west of Marseilles the Rhône – known

Flora and fauna
The first thing that springs to mind when thinking of Swiss flora is the profusion of beautiful Alpine flowers that accompany climbers and hikers right up to the snow-line. Everyone can contribute to keeping things that way: enjoy the flowers, but don't pick them. Many plants are strictly protected, anyhow, including the edelweiss, various kinds of gentian, the black nigritella, the orange lily, the Alpine columbine and the Alpine eryngo.

Swiss fauna is typically Central European. The chamois and the marmot are widespread in the Alps, and the number of ibex has increased rapidly in recent years. The golden eagle is a very rare sight these days.

The Brienzersee

romantically in its upper reaches as the 'Rotten' – flows out into the Golfe du Lion. The Ticino river is a tributary of the Po, which eventually reaches the Adriatic south of Venice.

Switzerland's 600 or so lakes are particularly attractive. Lac Léman (581sq km/224sq miles) is the largest, but even better known is Lake Luzern (Vierwaldstättersee; 114sq km/44sq miles) which is actually composed of seven smaller ones. The Brienzersee (29sq km/11sq miles) and Thunersee (48sq km/18sq miles) are separated only by the delta of the Lütschine river. To the northeast, Switzerland owns part of Bodensee (537sq km/207sq miles), part of Lago di Maggiore to the south (212sq km/81sq miles) and also Lago di Lugano (48sq km/18sq miles). The most important lakes in the Mittelland are the Lac de Neuchâtel (216sq km/83sq miles), the Zürichsee (89sq km/34sq miles), Bielersee (39sq km/15sq miles) and Zugersee (38sq km/15sq miles).

Rolling countryside in the Trogen region

CLIMATE AND WHEN TO GO

The Alps, in their function as a European watershed, exert a decisive influence on the Swiss climate. The regions north of the main Alpine ridge, including the Jura and the Mittelland, have a primarily Atlantic climate, while those to the south of the Alps enjoy far milder and sunnier Mediterranean climes. Alpine weather can vary considerably: there is often a lot of rain in the outer zones while the large valleys at the centre, such as those in Valais and the Engadine, remain dry and sunny. At elevations above 3,500m (11,480ft) all precipitation consists of snow. A warm, dry, stormy wind known as the *Föhn* usually occurs along the edge of the Alps, where high and low pressure areas meet. Its influence makes temperatures suddenly rise by several degrees. The *Föhn* not only melts large amounts of snow in spring, it also has an effect on people's moods: some grow depressed and complain about headaches, others become cheerful and hyperactive.

Switzerland can be visited at any time of year, but just before or just after peak season is ideal

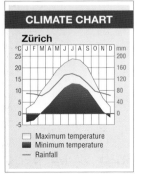

CLIMATE CHART

Zürich

	J	F	M	A	M	J	J	A	S	O	N	D	
°C													mm
25													200
20													160
15													120
10													80
5													40
0													0
-5													

☐ Maximum temperature
■ Minimum temperature
— Rainfall

– and cheaper, too. In spring, when the trees are in blossom, travel to Lac Léman, Valais or Ticino. The best time of year for mountain climbers and hikers is July to September, though finding accommodation can be difficult in the summer. Depending on the altitude, winter sports fans can usually find excellent snow conditions from December to April.

Below: idyllic Buchs
Bottom: drinking at Urnash cattle festival

THE PEOPLE AND THEIR LANGUAGES

Switzerland has approximately 7 million inhabitants, with a population density of roughly 169 inhabitants per sq km (105 per sq mile). This figure reveals nothing about the very varied distribution of population, however. For instance, only 10 percent of the entire Swiss population lives in the mountain cantons of Uri, Grisons, Ticino and Valais – which occupy 40 percent of the country's land. The less mountainous parts of the country have population densities varying between 213 (Thurgau) and 543 inhabitants per sq km. The proportion of foreigners amounts to about 16 percent, and as high as 37 percent in Geneva.

For several centuries Switzerland has succeeded in keeping four linguistic regions and several cultural peculiarities under one roof. A full 65 percent of the Swiss speak German, 18 percent French, 10 percent Italian and almost 1 percent

Romansh. The latter is kind of colloquial Latin, unrelated to Italian, still spoken in several valleys in Grisons and since 1938 officially considered the country's fourth language. Only 50,000 or so people still speak it, however. In eastern, northern and central Switzerland, *Schwyzerdütsch*, a dialect of Alemannian, is spoken; it varies a lot according to the different regions.

The cantons and the national government see it as their duty to protect the various regional languages and dialects, and to foster mutual understanding. The Federal Council is made up of representatives of all the linguistic groups. However, German and French are the official languages spoken in parliament.

POLITICS AND ADMINISTRATION

The Swiss Confederation is composed of 23 cantons, three of which have 'demicantons' – Zürich, Bern, Luzern, Uri, Schwyz, Unterwalden (demicantons: Obwalden, Nidwalden), Glarus, Zug, Fribourg, Solothurn, Basel (demicantons: Basel-Stadt, Basel-Land), Schaffhausen, Appenzell (demicantons: Inner-Rhoden, Ausser-Rhoden), St Gallen, Grisons, Aargau, Thurgau, Ticino, Vaud, Valais, Neuchâtel, Geneva and Jura.

The Swiss constitution provides both the confederation and cantons with the system of a demo-

> **Referendums**
> Switzerland's direct democracy results in numerous national referendums in which people have a direct say on important issues (and many not so important). Referenda are required for an amendment to the constitution; for a change in law demanded by a minimum of 50,000 voters nationwide, or by eight cantons; and for a popular initiative in which a new article to the constitution or a change of law is petitioned by at least 100,000 voters. But despite the power vested in the voter, and because of general economic and political stability, voter turnout is generally low.

Switzerland's charter of confederation, 1291

cratic republic in the form of direct or representative democracy. Power is devolved upwards from the 3,061 communities *(Gemeinde, commune)* each of which has a local council or municipal authority.

A Swiss citizen is first a citizen of the community (written in his passport) to which he belongs and which remains ultimately responsible for his welfare.

Below: in the William Tell chapel near Immensee
Bottom: the Monument de la Réformation, Geneva

RIGHTS AND RESPONSIBILITIES

The community has self-rule in all matters that are not the responsibility of the federal government or canton. Several communities make up a borough *(Bezirk, district)*. Next in line are the cantons, each of which has its own written constitution and is, in effect, a sovereign state subject to federal law. Each canton is responsible for its own civil service, citizenship, church matters, education, finances and income tax, fire service, labour department, land usage, law and order, libraries, public health, public transport, roads, water and electricity supply.

The federal government is directly responsible for the armed forces, civil, criminal and industrial law, currency, customs and taxes, fishing, forestry and hunting, foreign policy, hydroelectric power, monetary controls, pensions, post and communications and railways.

LEGISLATIVE POWER

Legislative power is exercised by the bicameral federal assembly *(Bundesversammlug, Assemblée Federale)*. Members are elected by all Swiss citizens aged 18 and older. The 200 seats on the National Council *(Nationalrat, Conseil National)* are divided up among the cantons according to population. In the Council of States *(Ständerat, Conseil des États)* the 20 full cantons have two representatives each, and each half-canton has one. Members of both chambers are non-professional politicians, and the smaller chamber has often acted as the conscience of the country.

ECONOMY

Banking
The cynical view of Swiss banking, and the wealth derived from it, owes something to pure envy but the intriguing question remains: how can this small, land-locked country with hardly any natural resources be so rich? As history shows, the origin of Swiss wealth was mainly based on two paradoxical factors: the booty of war, and neutrality, which was originally the basis on which best to sell impartial mercenary services.

Locarno's Grand Hotel

Switzerland is one of the richest countries in the world in terms of its gross national product, not only because its banks are so popular with investors. Two other factors are probably more important; its stable political situation and its hard currency. Rather tellingly, the service sector (banks, insurance, tourism) has become one of the mainstays of the economy, and brings in a lot of foreign currency. This compensates for the country's main disadvantages, namely its lack of raw materials and its lack of coastline. That Switzerland is still one of the most industrialised countries in the world is a tribute to its hard-working and resourceful population. Raw materials have to be imported for processing into high-quality products for resale, so Switzerland is very dependent on its exports. That is why it is a member of the World Trade Organisation (WTO) and the European Free Trade Association (EFTA). Through the latter it has had free trade agreements with the European Union (EU) and recently concluded free trade agreements with almost all nations of Central and Eastern Europe, the Mediterranean, and even more distant countries such as Mexico and Singapore.

Traditionally, Switzerland's most important industrial branches have been chemical and pharmaceutical (Basel), mechanical engineering (Zürich, Winterthur, Baden), watch-making (Jura, Geneva), and textiles (eastern Switzerland, Zürich). Today, food processing, and modern technologies such as biomedical engineering have also become important, and benefit greatly from a highly skilled workforce.

The principal agricultural product is milk, much of which is exported in one form or another, especially as cheese and chocolate. For a long time economic development, as well as folklore and culture, revolved around cows and herdsmen. The cattle drives to and from the Alps are still a popular theme in folk painting. Less well known but equally important for the economy and culture in some cantons has been wine production, the quality of which has improved recently.

SWITZERLAND AND EUROPE

In 1992 Switzerland voted against joining the European Economic Area (a kind of associated membership to the European Union). A double majority (popular votes plus cantons) was required. The sharp differences between the urban and rural areas of the country resulted in a great number of the small, rural cantons voting against membership. While 56 percent of Basel voted for, a full 74 percent of the rural canton of Uri voted against. The discrepancy between the linguistic regions was even greater. All the German-speaking cantons (with the exception of Basel) rejected the very notion of EEA and EU membership, while the western part of the country (centring on French-speaking Geneva) was clearly in favour. While the oldest, rural cantons wanted to remain independent, the industrial centres were interested in cooperating more closely with their neighbours.

Although Switzerland suffered a prolonged economic downturn in the 1990s and a number of international difficulties that were attributed by some to their political isolation, it did not translate into a popular move to seek EU membership. The government, however, decided to seek closer cooperation with the EU through a series of bilateral agreements that addressed such sensitive issues as the transit of trucks and the right of foreigners to live and work in Switzerland.

Below: a cheesemaker in Moleson
Bottom: a well-known brand

HISTORICAL HIGHLIGHTS

From 4000BC Pile dwellings appear around the lakes of the Mittelland.

From 400BC, Rhaetians enter the south. Celtic tribes settle the area between the Bodensee and Lac Léman.

58BC The most powerful Celtic tribe, the Helvetii are forced by Germanic tribes to migrate to Gaul. Julius Caesar pursues and defeats them at Bibracte (near Autun in Burgundy). The Helvetii are forced to return and allowed some self-government in what becomes Helvetia.

From 58BC With Helvetia as their buffer zone, the Romans fortify the Alpine passes, establish colonies and garrisons, and bring Roman ideas and civilisation to the region's inhabitants.

Turn of the 5th century AD With the Roman Empire falling, the Alemannians take northern Switzerland while the Burgundians seize the south, but in 534 the Franks conquer both. All of today's Switzerland, except Ticino, is united under a single power.

Early 7th century Irish monks St Columba and St Gallus, bring Christianity to Switzerland. The monastery in St Gallen, established in 614, later becomes one of the greatest seats of learning in Europe.

From 771 Under Charlemagne, Switzerland is divided into shires, from which many present cantons derive their names.

Early 9th century With the Treaty of Verdun, western Switzerland becomes part of the Kingdom of Burgundy.

1032 Burgundy and western Switzerland are incorporated into the Holy Roman Empire.

11th–13th centuries The gradual dissolution of the Holy Roman Empire enables the Houses of Habsburg and Savoy to gain influence. Bern, Zürich and several others become free imperial cities. Schwyz and Uri develop political autonomy.

1291 The three Forest Cantons of Uri, Schwyz and Unterwalden form the *Ewige Bund* (Everlasting League), thereby creating the nucleus of the Swiss Confederation. The oath sworn in the meadow at Rülti is the beginning of Swiss liberty, and the focus of folkloric tradition ever since, centring on the legend of William Tell.

1315 The peasant army of the Forest Cantons defeats the well-armed Habsburg army at Morgarten.

1322 Luzern is the first town to join the League, followed by Zürich, Zug and Bern in 1351–3.

1367–1471 Economic and social turmoil following the Black Death encourages other bids for freedom from feudalism. In Rhaetia, the people form the League of the House of God.

1386 The Habsburgs are defeated at the Battle of Sempach. The hero is Arnold von Winkelried, who throws himself on the Habsburg lances to allow foot soldiers to break through the lines.

1388 Glarus defeats the Austrian army at Näfels and joins the Swiss. With a total of eight states, the Confederation is firmly established.

15th century Switzerland begins to develop into a major European power. The Confederation grows rich on textiles.

1476 The Swiss annihilate the forces of the Burgundian duke, Charles the Bold, at Grandson.

1481 The Agreement of Stans allows Fribourg and Solothurn to join.

1499 After its victory over Austria and the Swabian League, the Swiss Confederation finally succeeds in breaking away from the empire.

1501–13 After a failed campaign against the French at Marignano, the Swiss proclaim absolute neutrality.

1518 The Catholic priest Huldrych Zwingli triggers the Swiss Reformation from Zürich by attacking both theological and social practices.

1523–8 The Reformation spreads quickly and splits the Confederation. Schaffhausen, Bern, Basel, Grisons and St Gallen join the new faith, while the Forest Cantons (now four), and Zug, Fribourg, Solothurn remain Catholic.

1536 Berne conquers the Vaud and with it both sides of Lac Léman, and Zwinglian worship is accepted throughout the new territory. French humanist John Calvin issues his *Institutes of the Christian Religion* from Basel and settles in Geneva.

mid-16th century onwards The Counter Reformation further divides the Swiss Confederation.

1555 Protestant families from Catholic areas find refuge in Zürich.

1572 French protestants flee to Switzerland after St Bartholomew massacre.

1616–48 Switzerland stays neutral in Thirty Years' War, and its sovereignty is recognised at the Peace of Westphalia

1712 The Peace of Aargau gives Protestants and Catholics equal rights. In the 18th century, the country remains agricultural, but city industries flourish, and watch-making begins to spread.

1798 Napoleon conquers Switzerland and makes it a unified state on the French model, called the Helvetian Republic.

1803 The 19 cantons regain partial sovereignty. The Vaid becomes French in 1810, emulating Geneva and Neuchâtel.

1815 After the fall of Napoleon, Geneva, Neuchâtel and Valais join the Confederation, now comprising 22 cantons.

1848 A new constitution is adopted making Switzerland a federal state.

1864 The Red Cross is founded by the Swiss humanitarian, Henri Duanant, and the first Geneva Convention is signed.

1870–1 Switzerland escapes entering the Franco–Prussian War.

1914–19/1939–45 Switzerland stays neutral during both world wars.

1971 Women gain the right to vote.

1978 Jura becomes the 23rd canton.

1986 Swiss vote against joining UN, afraid it might subvert neutrality policy.

1991 Switzerland's 700th anniversary.

1992 The Swiss vote no to joining EU

1997 Nazi Gold Scandal. Swiss banks found to have $57 million in dormant accounts, many opened by German Jews before World War II.

2002 The Swiss finally vote to become members of the UN.

Map on page 21

1: Basel

Basel (pop. 170,000), the second-largest city in Switzerland after Zürich, and capital of the canton of Basel-Stadt, lies between the Jura and the Black Forest on the site of an old Rhine crossing-point. The city has been influenced not only by the proximity of this great European river but also by its location at the junction of three countries: Switzerland, Germany and France. As a result it is not only cosmopolitan but also an important centre of trade and industry (chemicals and pharmaceuticals) as well as science and culture.

Preceding pages: Saanen
Below: Basel's Rathaus

Basel's university was founded by Pope Pius II in 1460, and one of its most famous students was the great humanist theologian, Erasmus of Rotterdam (1469–1536). The philosopher Friedrich Nietzsche (1844–1900) was a professor of philology here. Psychiatrist Carl Jung (1875–1961) studied medicine in the city. Of the many painters who worked in Basel, two deserve special mention: Hans Holbein the Younger (1497–1543) and Arnold Böcklin (1827–1901). Cultural life today keeps up the tradition: the city has 25 museums.

FASNACHT

Baselers' favourite time of year, however, is the *Fasnacht*, which begins on the Monday after Ash Wednesday with the legendary *Morgenstraich* (literally 'morning trick'). At exactly four o'clock in the morning all the lights in the city go out with Swiss precision, and thousands of lanterns are lit. Accompanied by the shrill sound of fife and drums, the procession of the *Cliquen* (*Fasnacht* organisations) begins. Each group has a special theme, usually political, and that evening current political issues are given sharply satirical treatment in pubs and bars across the city.

HISTORY

The Roman settlement of *Basilia* was first mentioned in 374. From the early 7th century it was a bishop's see. In the 10th century Basel became part of Burgundy, and in 1033 a part of the Holy Roman Empire. When the bridge across the Rhine was built in 1225 Basel began its steady rise to prominence as an important trading centre, and the severe earthquake of 1356 was only a temporary setback to its fortunes. The Council of Basel (1431–47) and the opening of the university (1460) established the city's reputation as a centre of culture and learning. In 1501 Basel joined the Swiss Confederation, and the Reformation arrived in 1529. In 1833, after civil war nearly broke out, the city was divided into two demicantons, Basel-Land and Basel-Stadt.

Star Attraction
• Basel's town centre

CITY TOUR

The Rhine, bending northwards, divides the city into two parts: Gross-Basel and Klein-Basel. On the southwestern bank is the ★★ **historic centre** of the city. Gross-Basel is largely free of traffic today, and is dominated by the Münster (cathedral). Its twin-towered silhouette can be seen to

A visionary negotiation
It was Basel's Lord Mayor, Johann Rudolf Wettstein, who had the vision, at the end of the Thirty Years' War, to negotiate Switzerland's groundbreaking and lasting neutrality.

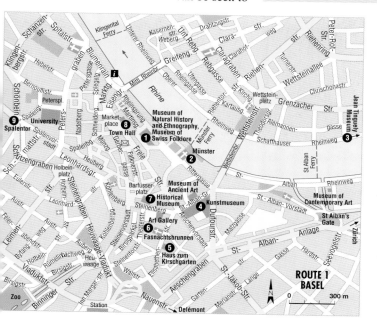

Map
on page
21

its best advantage from the Oberer Rheinweg on the opposite bank of the river, easily reached by taking the *Münsterfähre* (ferry). Notice the Swiss propensity for efficiency here: attached to a section of wire stretched across the river, the ship is propelled solely by the current – you can't get more ecologically sound than that. A short distance downriver is the Mittlerer Rheinbrücke. It was here that Bishop Heinrich von Thun built the first bridge in the area in 1225 – and he had to pawn the cathedral treasure to pay for it.

From the Mittlerer Rheinbrücke, a narrow, picturesque street known as the Rheinsprung leads back to the square in front of the Münster. Located in the equally picturesque Augustinergasse is the **Museum of Natural History and Ethnography** and the **Museum of Swiss Folklore** ❶ (open Tues–Sun 10am–5pm), with extensive collections (ceramics, feather head-dresses, masks, etc.) notably from Central America.

Not to be missed
The **Fondation Beyeler** at Baselstrasse 101 in the northeastern suburb of Riehen (open daily 10am–6pm, Wed until 8pm; www.beyeler.com) houses its collection of 20th-century masterpieces in an exceptional building by Renzo Piano. Permanent and special exhibits are intelligently presented in an elegant and peaceful setting.

THE MÜNSTER

Just a few steps further on is the red-sandstone façade of the ★★ **Münster** ❷ or former cathedral. This 12th-century structure is basically a late Romanesque basilica with transepts and an ambulatory, but the Gothic influence is unmistakeable. The west façade was redesigned after a fire in

The Münster

1258, and funeral chapels were added shortly afterwards. After the severe earthquake of 1356 destroyed the towers, vault and crypt, reconstruction took place in the style of the time.

This development can be traced in the wonderful statuary outside the building. Beginning with the late Romanesque choir capitals to the ★ **St Gallus Portal** (*Galluspforte*, c. 1180) in the north transept, considered the most important late Romanesque sculpted portal in Switzerland, and leading on to the archivolts and statues on the western façade, which was placed there after the earthquake of 1356. Subsequent additions are the late Gothic towers (1430 and 1500), the pulpit (1486) and finally the two 15th-century southern cloisters.

A TRIO OF MUSEUMS

Paper manufacturing began in the St Alban quarter of the city in the 15th century, and its history is well documented in the **Basel Paper Museum** (open Tues–Sun 2–5pm). The new **Jean Tinguely Museum ❸** (open Wed–Sun 11am–7pm), located a bit further upstream, is dedicated to art work by the Swiss kinetic artist Jean Tinguely (1925–91), who is famous for his dramatic machine-like sculptures.

Nearby is the Gothic church of St Alban, and also the Museum of Contemporary Art, part of the famous ★★ **Kunstmuseum ❹** (open Tues–Sun 10am–5pm). In 1661 the city purchased the Basilius Amerbach collection, and it formed the basis for what today is the oldest and also one of the greatest public portrait galleries in Europe. Auguste Rodin's *Les Bourgeois de Calais* welcomes visitors at the entrance.

Upper Rhenish and Swiss painting of the 15th and 16th centuries is particularly well represented here, with works by several excellent artists, including Konrad Witz. The museum contains the most comprehensive collection of ★ **Holbeins** in the world. The Cubist collection is also very extensive, with works by Picasso, Braque, Gris and Paul Klee.

Star Attractions
• the Münster
• the Kunstmuseum

Below: Holbein's portrait of Dorothea Kannengeisser
Bottom: Klee's Villa R

Map on page 21

In the Haus zum Kirschgarten

PAST AND PRESENT

A good place to experience what life was like in Basel in the 18th and 19th centuries is the ★ **Haus zum Kirschgarten ❺** (open Tues–Sun 10am–5pm), a mansion built in 1777, with a fine collection of faïence, porcelain and old toys.

In great contrast is the popular **Fasnachtsbrunnen ❻**, a fountain created in 1977 by Jean Tinguely. Bizarre mechanical devices spout streams of water and move about in the large pool.

The Barfüsserkirche, in the square of the same name, houses the ★ **Historical Museum ❼** (open Wed–Mon 10am–5pm). This austere-looking building is a good example of early 14th-century Mendicant Order architecture. The extensive collection here includes prehistoric finds, religious and secular medieval art, goldsmiths' masterpieces that formed part of the cathedral treasure, tapestries, Renaissance and baroque artefacts and several ancient weapons.

FROM THE MARKET PLACE TO THE ZOO

At the heart of the Old Town is the market place, the **Marktplatz**; the flower and vegetable stalls are usually buzzing with activity during the daytime. The most striking feature is the colourfully painted, red sandstone façade of the ★ **Town Hall** (Rathaus) ❽ (guided tours available). Built between 1507 and 1513, it was extended a century later, and the tower was added between 1898 and 1904. The clock (1511–12) is the work of a local craftsman known simply as Wilhelm.

The ★ **Spalentor ❾**, the finest of the remaining town gates, with two battlemented towers, is a locally well known sight. German philosopher Friedrich Nietzsche lived at No. 47 in the adjacent Schützengraben from 1869 to 1879.

For families, a good excursion from Basel is to the **Zoo** (open May–Aug: daily 8am–6.30pm; Mar–April and Sept–Oct: till 6pm; Nov–Feb til 5.30pm). The zoo is affectionately known as the *Zolli*, and is an ideal place to take small children – for all the obvious reasons, plus the fact that you can stroke many of the animals.

2: Bern

Bern (pop. 133,000), at the heart of Switzerland, right on the German–French linguistic divide, is the capital of the canton of the same name and the capital of the Confederation, but is neither its cultural nor its industrial centre. Despite this, the city seems far more quintessentially Swiss to visitors than Geneva or Zürich. This is partly because of the local German dialect, known as *Bärndütsch*, but also because of the inhabitants' legendary slowness. Although this is often mocked by inhabitants of other parts of Switzerland, it has its positive effects as well – the people of Bern believe in leaving things alone. One obvious benefit is the beauty of the historic Old Town, still almost completely intact.

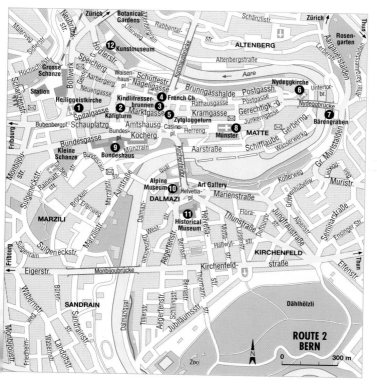

ROUTE 2
BERN

0   300 m

Map on page 25

HISTORY

Bern was founded in 1191 by Duke Berchtold V of Zähringen and became a free imperial city in 1218. Its independence was confirmed by the victory of Laupen (1339) when the Burgundians and the town of Fribourg were defeated. Bern joined the Confederation in 1353 and soon began to expand: in 1415 it annexed the Aargau, and after its conquest of the Vaud in 1536 it became the largest city-state north of the Alps.

Farmers and burghers tried unsuccessfully to rebel against the might of the ruling patricians in 1653 and 1749 respectively; the first real shock the city suffered was in 1798, when the French plundered the municipal Treasury. Bern became the capital of the Swiss Confederation in 1848. Among the scholars and artists Bern has produced over the centuries, special mention should be made of the natural scientist, Albrecht von Haller (1708–77), and also Switzerland's greatest painter, Ferdinand Hodler (1853–1918).

A city's name
Horace Walpole explained the significance of Bern's bear emblem in a letter written in 1766: *The most faire Bern hath the name of Beares in the Dutch tongue, because Berthold Duke of Zeringen, being to build the Citie, and going forth to hunt, thought good to give it the name of the first beast he should meete and kill.*

Art Nouveau detail on the Musik Konservatorium

CITY TOUR

The arcades are the most noticeable feature of Bern's ★★★ **Old Town** *(Altstadt)*. Other typical sights are the numerous fountains, complete with statues, most of which date from the 16th century. The main axis of the historic centre runs from the

modern railway station to the Nydeggbrücke, and is made up of Spitalgasse, Marktgasse, Kramgasse and Gerechtigkeitsgasse. These streets constitute the most important architectural ensemble in the whole of Switzerland.

Construction of the medieval town took place in four phases between 1191 and 1346. The original centre, with the old Zähringer fortress (destroyed in 1270), extended from the Nydeggasse to the Kreuzgasse. During the first phase the town spread westwards out as far as the Zytgloggeturm, then after 1256 as far as the Käfigturm. Finally, the outer 'new town' section along the Spitalgasse was added.

At the beginning of the Spitalgasse is the **Heiliggeistkirche** ❶, built between 1726 and 1729 and probably the most important Protestant baroque church in Switzerland. The bright interior is lent extra character by the sandstone columns and the long gallery.

THE BÄRENPLATZ

The street café terraces in the Bärenplatz, with the eye-catching, 16th-century **Käfigturm** ❷, are just the place to sit and relax on sunny afternoons. The most original of all Bern's numerous fountains can be seen in the middle of the Kornhausplatz: the **Kindlifresserbrunnen** ❸, which was erected in 1546 and originally designed to frighten small children into submission. It probably doesn't scare many of them these days.

The largest building in the square is the Kornhaus (1711–18), a typical example of Bernese high baroque. Behind it, the **French Church** ❹, built at the end of the 13th century in austere Mendicant Order Gothic, was given a lot of baroque additions around 1754. The rood screen inside, with its fresco decoration, dates from 1495.

THE ZYTGLOGGETURM

The most well-known sight in Bern, however, is probably the 12th-century ★ **Zytgloggeturm** ❺, formerly the western gate when the medieval

Star Attraction
• **Old Town**

Below: Marktgasse
Bottom: the Zytgloggeturm astronomical clock

Map
on page
25

> **The Matte**
> The land in the centre of Bern falls steeply on three sides down to the River Aare. This area forms the 'lower town' where the social level of life was once lower as well. Known as The Matte, this was once a workers' and artisans' quarter, and is now particularly favoured by artists and other creative people.

A Bern bear

town was extended. Its walls were originally 3m (10ft) thick; the tower has undergone several alterations over the years. The much-admired chiming astronomical clock (1527–30) was added by Kaspar Brunner. Just before the hour, crowds gather to watch several figures whirr into action.

The broad Kramgasse is perhaps the finest street in the city. The row of baroque façades is harmonious, and two flag-bedecked, 16th-century fountains provide an attractive contrast. Albert Einstein lived at No. 19 from 1902 to 1909. Today the house includes a small **museum** (open Feb–Nov: Tues–Fri 1–5pm, Sat noon–4pm), full of memorabilia.

BRIDGES AND BEARS

The main axis comes to an end in Gerechtigkeitsgasse, which ends up at the **Nydeggkirche ❻**, a late Gothic structure built on the foundations of the old Zähringer fortress. Gerechtigkeitsgasse leads to the 25-m (82-ft) Nydeggbrücke, which spans the Aare. The oldest bridge in the city is the adjacent, stone-built Untertorbrücke (1461); until 1844 it was the only means of crossing the river.

On the opposite bank on the right is the ★ **Bärengraben ❼**, or bear-pit, which is nearly always surrounded by onlookers. The bears are as much a part of Bern as the gondolas are of Venice. It was in 1513 that the Bernese troops brought back a real bear as booty after the Battle of Novara, and since then they have been a permanent feature of the city.

THE MÜNSTER AND THE BUNDESHAUS

Towering above the roofs of the old town is the 100-m (328-ft) high spire of the ★★ **Münster ❽**. This enormous church measures 84m (275ft) by 34m (110ft), and took a full 150 years to complete. Its spire, modelled after the one on Ulm cathedral in Germany, dates only from 1893. The ★ **main portal** (1490–1500) with its wealth of sculpture is an important architectural feature; the rendition of the *Last Judgement* is particularly good. Highlights inside the church include the famous ★ **stained-glass windows** above the altar.

The ★ **Bundeshaus** (Federal Palace) ❾ (guided tours available) is a Florentine Renaissance style building. The central section, with a dome, built between 1894 and 1902, is the seat of the bicameral Swiss parliament (*Bundesversammlung*). There's a good view of the Aare, with the Kirchenfeldbrücke across to the left. It connects the old town with the Helvetiaplatz, where there are several interesting museums.

ALPS, ARCHAEOLOGY AND ART

On the left is the Kunsthalle, and opposite is the **Swiss Alpine Museum** ❿ (open Mon 2–5pm, Tues–Sun 10am–5pm), documenting the history and exploration of the Alps. The **Historical Museum** ⓫ (open Tues–Sun 10am–5pm, Wed 10am–8pm) contains some fascinating archaeological collections. The ★★ **Kunstmuseum** ⓬ (open Tues 10am–9pm, Wed–Sun 10am–5pm) documents Bernese and Swiss art from medieval times to the present. It also contains 14th-century Italian works, 19th-century French masters and the renowned Paul Klee collection, with over 40 of his paintings, 200 watercolours and more than 2,000 drawings. Klee (1879–1940) was born just outside Bern.

Star Attractions
• the Münster
• the Kunstmuseum

Below: the Bundeshaus
Bottom: the Last Judgement

Map on page 30

3: Geneva

Geneva (Genève, pop. 168,000), capital of the tiny canton of the same name (pop. 387,000), is far more cosmopolitan than any other Swiss city – not just because of its geographic location right next to the French border but also because it is the European seat of the United Nations, WTO, EFTA (the European Free Trade Association) and several other international organisations. The population is just as diverse; 37 percent are foreigners.

International Geneva
Geneva's rise to the world-famous conference centre it is today began in 1871: a court of arbitration was held in the Town Hall during a row about the sinking of the battle cruiser *Alabama* in the American Civil War. In 1876, in commemoration, US officers handed in their swords, the metal of which was recast into the form of a ploughshare that is still displayed in the Town Hall's *Salle Alabama*.

HISTORY

The earliest traces of settlement here date from the Stone Age. In 120BC the Celtic settlement became part of the Roman province of Gallia Narbonensis. Converted to Christianity in the 4th century, the town was conquered in 443 by the Burgundians, who made it their capital. It was later taken by the Franks and in 1032 became a free imperial city under the Holy Roman Empire.

After the Reformation arrived in 1532, Jean Calvin (1509–64) made Geneva the centre of Protestantism. In 1584 the city made an alliance

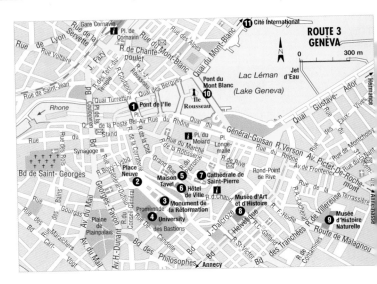

with Bern and Zürich, and in 1798 it was occupied by the French. After the fall of Napoleon local patriots pressed for independence, and in 1815 Geneva joined the Confederation as its twenty-second canton.

Geneva is famous as the home of two great philosophers and writers – Voltaire (1694–1778), and Jean-Jacques Rousseau (1712–78), whose writing profoundly affected the French Revolution. Philanthropic businessman Henri Dunant founded the International Red Cross here in 1864, and elevated the Swiss flag to the international symbol of humanity.

Below: base of Geneva's famous Jet d'Eau fountain
Bottom: Rousseau's birthplace

CITY TOUR

The best place to start a tour of the city is the **Pont de l'Ile ❶**. The Rue de la Cerraterie, harmoniously laid out in the 19th century and today one of Geneva's most elegant shopping streets, leads to the **Place Neuve ❷** with the Grand Théâtre, the Conservatory of Music, and the Musée Rath (which stages alternating exhibitions). The Place Neuve opens into the tree-lined Promenade des Bastions. On the left is the **Monument de la Réformation ❸**, erected in 1917. At the centre of this 100-m (328-ft) long, unadorned wall are the enormous likenesses of eminent leaders of the movement – Farel, Calvin, de Bèze and Knox.

The neoclassical **university ❹**, built between 1868 and 1872, developed from an academy originally founded by Calvin. It contains the ★ **Musée Jean-Jacques Rousseau** (open Mon–Fri 9am–noon and 2–5pm, Sat 9am–noon), with a collection of manuscripts and memorabilia documenting his life.

THE VIEILLE VILLE

Across the Promenade des Bastions on a small rise is the **Vieille Ville**, or old town. The narrow streets between the Place Bel-Air and the cathedral are ideal for a stroll, and several fine old buildings can be admired, including houses in the Grand Rue, dating from the 15th to 18th centuries.

JEAN-JACQUES
ROUSSEAU
EST NÉ
DANS
CETTE MAISON
LE 28 JUIN 1712

FACADE REMANIÉE

Map on page 30

Jean-Jacques Rousseau was born at No. 40 on 28 June 1712.

The oldest residential building in the city is the **Maison Tavel ❺**, mentioned in documents as long ago as 1303; its inner courtyard is particularly delightful. Today the building houses the **Altstadtmuseum** (open Tues–Sun 10am–5pm), which has a good scale model showing what the city looked like in 1850.

The ★ **Hôtel de Ville ❻** (Town Hall) was built in several stages between 1440 and 1707. This is where the first Geneva Convention was signed on 22 August 1864. The attractive Renaissance courtyard makes a pleasant venue for open-air classical concerts in the summer months. Note the square tower, inside which the different floors are connected by a ramp rather than stairs.

VIEWS AND OVERVIEWS

The highest point of the Vieille Ville is the ★ **Cathédrale de Saint-Pierre ❼**, a three-aisled basilica dating from the late 12th century. The church was started in Romanesque style and completed during the Gothic period. A neoclassical pillared portico was added to the main façade during the 18th century, principally to stop the front wall from collapsing. Some of the sculpture inside the church is unique in Switzerland.

Looking for answers
CERN, the European Laboratory for Particle Physics, is a part of international Geneva. Here, 3,000 full-time employees and 6,000 visiting experts from all over the world explore the inner structure of matter, to see 'what makes the planet tick'.

The largest LEP or Large Electron Positron Storage Ring, completed in 1989, is 27km (17 miles) long.

Inside the Hôtel de Ville

Next door is the 15th-century **Temple d'Auditoire** (open Mon–Sat 10am–noon, 2–5pm, Sun 11.10am–12.30pm, 1.30–5pm), which was used by Calvin and de Bèze as an auditorium.

The most important museum in Geneva is the ★★ **Musée d'Art et d'Histoire** ❽ (open Tues–Sun 10am–5pm), with major art and art history collections. They feature Egyptian, Greek, Etruscan and Roman exhibits, alongside prehistoric finds from the Geneva area and several medieval religious artefacts – including a fine ★ **altar** (1444) by Konrad Witz. The art gallery here gives a good general overview of painting in Geneva from the 15th century to the present day.

Another museum that is worth seeing is the **Musée d'Histoire Naturelle** ❾ (open Tues– Sun 9.30am–5pm) on the Route de Malagnou, with fascinating zoological, palaentological, geological and mineralogical collections. The villa next door houses the fascinating **Musée d'Horlogerie** (Clock Museum; closed Tues).

FURTHER AFIELD

The western bank of the river can be reached via the broad and busy **Pont du Mont-Blanc** ❿. Alongside the pompous hotels on the Quai du Mont-Blanc is the bombastic Mausoleum of Duke Charles II of Brunswick. He spent his final years in Geneva and donated his fortune to the city.

To the north is the **Cité International** ⓫ where numerous international organisations are based. At its centre is the ★ **Palais des Nations** (tours daily 10am–noon and 2–4pm; July and Aug: 9am–6pm), built as the headquarters of the League of Nations between 1929 and 1937 and today the European headquarters of the UN.

As well as the ever-popular boat trips on the lake, another good excursion is to the picturesque little town of **Hermance**, founded in the 13th century, 14km (8 miles) away on the eastern shore. The trip could be combined with a detour to the Fondation Bodmer (Thurs 2–5pm) in **Cologny**, famous for its collection of ancient manuscripts, early books and first editions.

Star Attraction
• **Musée d'Art et d'Histoire**

Below: a Giacometti self-portrait
Bottom: the Soviet monument at the UN

Map below

4: Luzern

Luzern (pop. 63,000), on Lake Luzern (the Vierwaldstättersee in German), with quaint, covered wooden bridges across the Reuss river, Alpine peaks in the distance, and paddle steamers on the lake, is a picture-postcard idyll. It has been a centre of tourism for well over a century, and is particularly popular with the British. In peak season cafés fill to bursting and streets are packed with cars – which is why most of the local population moves out in the summer.

HISTORY

Luzern, which grew up around a Benedictine convent, dates from 1178; after the Gotthard route opened in the 13th century it became an important trading centre. In 1332 it joined the alliance of the Forest Cantons which, in July 1386, defended their independence at the Battle of Sempach. Like other conservative enclaves, it remained a Catholic stronghold, and later became a centre of the Counter-Reformation. From 1798 to 1799, after the collapse of the Confederation, it was the seat of the Helvetian government.

The secret capital
Many consider Luzern to be the secret capital of Switzerland: if Bern is the head, and Zürich the hand, then Luzern can certainly pride itself on being the heart of the country.

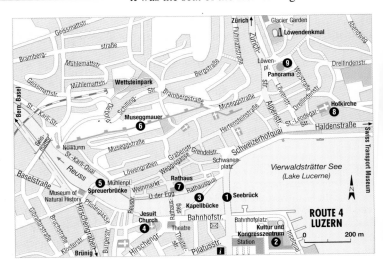

TOURING THE TOWN

The best view of the town, the lake and the mountains is from the broad and busy **Seebrücke** ❶, which connects the Bahnhofplatz with the Schweizerhof Quay. The highest peaks in the distance are Pilatus (2,129m/6,980ft) and Rigi (1,798m/5,899ft), and they seem incredibly close during times of *Föhn (see page 11)*. A recent addition to the city's skyline (next to the station) is the modern **Kultur- und Kongresszentrum** ❷, designed by the trendy French architect, Jean Nouvel. It houses a large concert hall and the Museum of Art.

Luzern's most famous landmark is the **★★ Kapellbrücke** ❸, spanning the Reuss at an angle below the Seebrücke. The oldest covered wooden bridge in Europe, it was built at the beginning of the 14th century as part of the town's fortifications. In 1993 it was severely damaged in a fire, and the magnificent fresco cycle that hung from its rafters was destroyed. The octagonal water tower, formerly a bastion of the ancient fortifications, was spared, however. The bridge has been almost entirely reconstructed, and is still the most popular site in town.

A little further up the Reuss, on the south bank, are the twin towers of the **Jesuit Church** ❹. Built between 1666 and 1669, it is the largest baroque building in Switzerland; the interior, with rich stucco decoration by the Wessobrunn school, is particularly impressive. Right next door to the church is the Rittersche Palast, a Florentine Renaissance structure once owned by the Jesuits; since 1804 it has been the Regierungsgebäude and accommodates cantonal offices. The building's graceful Tuscan columns are highly attractive.

THE SPREUERBRÜCKE

Next comes the second of Luzern's covered bridges, the **★ Spreuerbrücke** ❺. Built in 1408, it contains several paintings of the *Dance of Death* (1626–35) by Kaspar Meglinger. On the Kasernenplatz next to the entrance to the bridge is the former orphanage, a neoclassical building dating

Star Attraction
• Kapellbrücke

Below: the Jesuit Church
Bottom: the Kapellbrücke

Map
on page
34

from 1811, which today houses an interesting **Natural History Museum** (open Tues–Sat 10am–noon and 2–5pm, Sun 10am–5pm).

From the Spreuerbrücke there's a fine view of the old part of town north of the Reuss, the so-called Gross-Stadt, and of the nine-towered ★ **Museggmauer ⑥** (sometimes open to visitors in summer). Erected around 1400 it is 870m (2,850ft) in length; it not only rounds off the old part of town visually but is also one of the best-preserved fortifications in the whole of Switzerland.

THE RATHAUS AND THE HOFKIRCHE

At the centre of the historic town centre is the Weinmarkt, surrounded by the frescoed façades of several patrician houses. It leads on to the **Kornmarkt** and the massive ★ **Rathaus** (Town Hall) **⑦**. Built at the beginning of the 17th century, its façade was strongly influenced by the Florentine early Renaissance style, while the hipped, saddleback roof reflects local traditions. The **Am-Rhyn-Haus** (open daily 10am–6pm) next door was built in 1618 and contains a small but exquisite **Picasso collection** with works from 1953 to 1969.

To the east of the city the twin, tapering Gothic spires of the ★ **Hofkirche ⑧** are unmistakable. They surmount the towers of a basilica that burnt down in 1633. This sturdy late Renaissance

For art lovers
The Rosengart Collection and the accompanying Picasso Museum are two of Luzern's newest and most impressive offerings for admirers of late 19th-century and early 20th-century masters (open April–Oct: daily 10am–6pm, Nov–Mar: daily 11am–4pm).

The Löwendenkmal

structure is surrounded by an arcaded churchyard similar to an Italian Campo Santo, with a good view of the lake. Beneath the church is the Rothenburger Haus, built around 1500, the oldest complete wooden house in Switzerland.

LÖWENPLATZ

Löwenstrasse leads to the Löwenplatz with the popular ★ **Panorama** ❾ by Edouard Castres, depicting the retreat into Switzerland of General Bourbaki's French army in 1871. Close by is the famous **Löwendenkmal**, or Lion Monument. Designed by Danish sculptor, Thorvaldsen, and carved in 1821, it commemorates the heroic Swiss Guards who fell protecting the French king Louis XVI during the storming of the Tuileries in 1792. Beside it is the entrance to the **Gletschergarten** (Glacier Garden), an excavation site of geological and palaeontological interest with fossils, minerals and natural holes, some over 9m (30ft) deep.

Below and bottom: a transport museum exhibit

EXCURSIONS FROM LUZERN

Luzern is a good starting-point for several excursions. The remarkable ★★**Swiss Transport Museum** (open April–Oct: daily 10am–6pm, Nov–Mar: daily 10am–5pm) out in Luzern's eastern suburbs has been the most popular family museum in Switzerland ever since it opened in 1959. The innumerable exhibits – most of them original – document every conceivable kind of transport and communication, including road and rail transport, aviation, space travel and postal services. The planetarium lets visitors experience a space-flight simulation. There is also an IMAX Cinema in the museum's grounds.

Classical music enthusiasts should definitely visit ★ **Haus Tribschen** (open mid-March–31 Oct: Tues–Sun 10am–6pm) to the south of the city, where Richard Wagner lived from 1866 to 1872 before moving to Bayreuth. This is where his *Tribschen Idyll*, later renamed the *Siegfried Idyll*, was composed and first performed; he also wrote his *Meistersinger* here, completed *Siegfried*

Map on page 34

and began *Götterdämmerung*. The young Nietzsche visited Tribschen numerous times. Exhibits here include Wagner's grand piano, his velvet jacket and a beret.

LAKE LUZERN AND PILATUS

A visit to Luzern is incomplete without a trip across ★★ **Lake Luzern** (boats leave from the quay near the station). The lake (114sq km/44sq miles) is not only beautiful, it is central to Swiss history, and amid the magnificent mountain scenery it's easy to imagine the heroic freedom-fighters from Uri, Schwyz and Unterwalden who inspired Schiller to write his *William Tell*.

★★ **Pilatus** (2,128m/7,000ft) offers one of the best panoramic views in the northern Alps. From the small town of Kriens a cable car goes up to just below the summit. Even more scenic is a trip on Europe's steepest **rack railway** from Alpnachstad to the Pilatus-Kulm (2,078m/6,800ft).

Another good excursion from Luzern is to ★ **Engelberg**, 35km (21 miles) from the city and easily reached along a fast road. There's also a train connection. Engelberg is a popular holiday resort that offers tennis, hang-gliding and even summer skiing on the Titlis (3,239m/10,600ft). Unlike some resorts, the town is quite level and not too strenuous to walk around.

International music festival
This prestigious festival of classical music began in 1938 with a concert by Italian conductor Arturo Toscanini in the grounds of Richard Wagner's Haus Tribschen, and now draws the world's best orchestras and soloists to venues all around town from mid-August to mid-September (www.lucernemusic.ch).

Haus Tribschen

5: Zürich

Zürich (pop. 360,000) is in the Swiss Mittelland, roughly halfway between the Rhine and the Alps at the northwestern end of Lake Zürich (the Zürich-see). It is not Switzerland's capital, but it is by far the largest city in the country and is seen, particularly by its inhabitants, as the pulsating heart that gives life to the whole country. Its position as the country's financial and economic centre is undisputed, but the city also holds many attractions for those travelling purely for pleasure. The shops along the Bahnhofstrasse are justifiably world-famous, as are the theatres, restaurants and museums. And, of course, there are always the delights of the Zürichsee. In 2002 it was rated the most desirable city in the world in which to live (with Geneva and Bern also figuring in the top 10).

HISTORY

The Romans built a military camp on the site of today's Lindenhof around 58BC, and the market town of Turicum sprang up under their protection. In 1218 Zürich became a free imperial city, and joined the Confederation in 1351. During the 16th century it was the centre of the Reformation in German-speaking Switzerland, largely due to reformer Huldrych Zwingli (1484–1531). The constitution of 1831 put an end to the privileges enjoyed by the urban population, and the city's fortifications were removed shortly afterwards.

CITY TOUR

The best starting point for a tour of Zürich is the busy **Bahnhofplatz** ❶. At the centre of the square and looking rather isolated among the traffic is the fountain memorial to Alfred Escher (1819–82), initiator of the Gotthard railway.

Beyond the Bahnhof (railway station), on the promontory between the Limmat and the Sihl, is the fortress-like ★★ **Swiss National Museum** (Schweizerische Landesmuseum) ❷ (open Tues–Sun 10.30am–5pm). It contains the most

Map on page 40

Star Attraction
•**Swiss National Museum**

Below: a Swiss chocolate shop
Bottom: the Swiss National Museum

Map below

Good food on a budget
When you are hungry and on a budget in Switzerland, eating a lunchtime fixed price menu is your best bet. You will find a wide range of restaurants (including some that are double the price in the evening) that will offer delicious specials of the day.

comprehensive collection of Swiss historical and cultural artefacts in the country, displayed in more than 100 rooms. The exhibitions documenting prehistoric Switzerland and the Roman occupation are particularly good, as are the collections of religious and profane medieval art. A series of rooms have been furnished in the styles of the 15th to 18th centuries, and the weapons collection hall contains frescoes by Ferdinand Hodler. The stained glass collection is also worth a visit.

SHOPPING AND SPIRES

Zürich's 1.2-km (¾-mile) long, partly pedestrianised **Bahnhofstrasse** leads from the Bahnhofplatz to the Bürkliplatz by the lake. Most of the

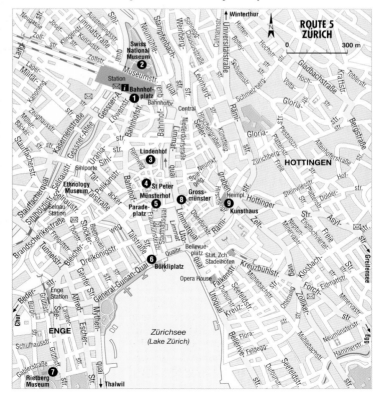

street dates from 1864 to 1867, when the medieval fortifications were dismantled. This elegant shopping street – known as 'Switzerland's shop window' – is one of the most famous in the world.

The old part of Zürich is less hectic. Although much of its ancient substance has been disfigured by modern planning, it still has its delightful corners and picturesque squares. The section on the west bank of the Limmat is dominated by the **Lindenhof ❸**, a natural moraine where the city was first settled; there is an attractive view across the river and the eastern part of Zürich.

The mighty spire of **St Peter's Church ❹** stands out against the rooftops. The clock-face (1538), almost 8.7m (28ft) in diameter, is the largest in Europe. Inside, on the northern wall, is the tomb of theologian Johann Kaspar Lavater (1741–1801), pastor of this church for 23 years, who invented the science of physiognomics.

MÜNSTERHOF

The ★ **Münsterhof ❺** is widely considered to be the most attractive square in the old part of Zürich. At its northwestern end is the Zünfthaus Zur Waag (1637), while the eastern side is dominated by the ★★ **Zunfthaus Zur Meise**. This magnificent rococo structure, built for the city's wine guild in 1752, houses the Ceramics Collection of the Swiss National Museum *(see pages 39–40)*. The south side is overlooked by the ★ **Fraumünster** with its tall spire. Although this 13th-century church has retained its Romanesque choir, it has been greatly altered over the centuries. Marc Chagall's ★ **stained-glass windows** can be seen from the choir and the transept.

BARGAINS, VIEWS AND ORIENTAL ART

If the weather is fine there are two good reasons to visit the **Bürkliplatz ❻** and the **Quaibrücke**. One is the flea market held here every Saturday during the summer, and the other is the pleasant view from the bridge across the lake to the Alpine peaks in the far distance.

Star Attraction
• **Zunfthaus Zur Meise**

Below: shopping along Bahnhofstrasse
Bottom: the Rietberg Museum

Map on page 40

Those interested in Oriental and African art will enjoy a visit to the Villa Wesendonck (1857), which, since 1952, has housed the ★ **Rietberg Museum** ❼ (open Tues–Sun 10am–5pm, Wed 10am–8pm). The collections on display here include Indian and Chinese works, but there are also some from Africa and Polynesia.

DISTINCTIVE LANDMARKS

If you look down the Limmat River from the Quaibrücke, two buildings beside the Grossmünster stand out distinctively: one is the towerless, Gothic **Wasserkirche** (1484), the other is the mighty, late Renaissance **Rathaus** (1698).

On the Limmat quay are two more historic buildings that document the former importance of the Zürich guilds: the **Zunfthaus Zur Saffran** (1723), where the grocers' guild used to meet, and the **Zunfthaus zur Zimmerleuten** (1708), the carpenters' guild house, with its oriel windows.

The city's most famous landmark is the ★★ **Grossmünster** ❽ with its two conspicuous towers. Before the Reformation this Protestant church belonged to a canonical foundation that, according to legend, was founded by Charlemagne, a statue of whom can be seen by the south wall, facing the Limmat. From the tower named after him, the **Karlsturm** (open in summer)

Switzerland's most famous radical

A highly educated man, greatly influenced by Erasmus' humanism, and passionate about individual freedom, Pastor Huldrych Zwingli (1484–1531) sought to reform not only the church but all of Swiss society.

The Zunfthaus zur Zimmerleuten

there's a good view of the surrounding old town. The Romanesque Grossmünster was probably founded around 1100, and was completed in the mid-13th century. The rich ornamentation on the northern portal and on the pillars in the nave dates from around 1180, and the crypt contains the remains of several medieval frescoes.

Star Attractions
- Grossmünster
- Kunsthaus

FAMOUS RESIDENTS

Several famous names are associated with the old part of Zürich on the right bank of the Limmat: Georg Büchner (1813–37) the Expressionist playwright, lived in the Spiegelgasse for the last years of his short life; and Vladimir Ilich Ulyanov (1870 1924), better known as Lenin, was also resident here. The Dada movement was founded here in 1916, overturning previously unquestioned strictures of style and order, not only in the arts but across society. Another famous Zürich resident, although not associated with this area, was educationalist Heinrich Pestalozzi (1746–1827).

Above the Hirschgraben – formerly the city wall – are the monumental Federal Institute of Technology (with an important graphics collection) and the university (with a zoological and palaeontological museum). Switzerland has a long tradition of excellence in the sciences: the Federal Institute of Technology has produced more Nobel Prize winners than any other scientific school in the world.

Below: Giacometti stained glass in the Grossmünster Bottom: Ruisdael's View of Haarlem

SPLENDID COLLECTIONS

The ★★**Kunsthaus** ❾ (open Tues–Thur 10am–9pm, Fri–Sun 10am–5pm) on Heimplatz is one of the largest portrait galleries in Switzerland. It also contains several collections of antique and medieval sculpture. The medieval painting section exhibits works by Hans Asper and many Dutch 17th-century masters (Rubens, Hals and Rembrandt). Swiss 19th- and 20th-century painting is represented by Arnold Böcklin, Ferdinand Hodler, Cuno Amiet, Felix Vallotton and Giovanni Segantini.

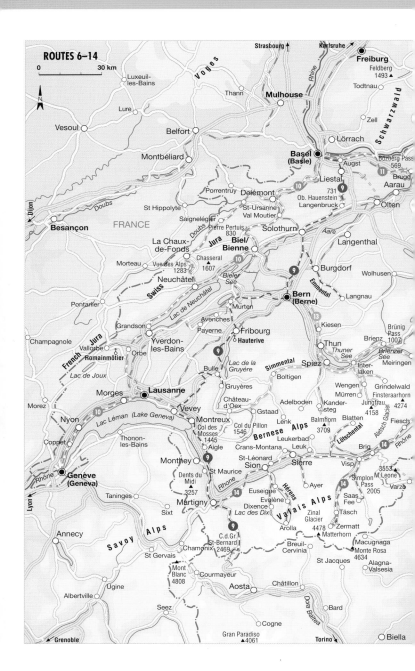

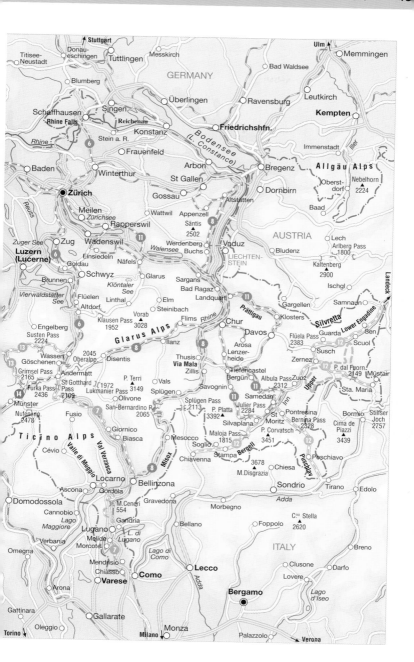

Map on pages 44–5

Schaffhausen bombed
Schaffhausen, the only sizable part of Switzerland on the north side of the Rhine, was the only part to be bombed during World War II. Allied forces said it was a mistake, but there were allegations that Schaffhausen's munitions industries were supplying arms to the Nazis in breach of Swiss neutrality. Records which could shed light on the matter are still sealed and secret.

6: Into the Mountains

Schaffhausen – Zürich – Schwyz – Andermatt (163km/101 miles)

The classic route south, whether towards Ticino or further south into Italy, leads either via the St Gotthard Pass or through the Gotthard Tunnel. This route is a busy one, and traffic jams often occur at peak hours despite the motorways. To enjoy a slower version of the trip and soak up the landscape, switch to the cantonal roads. There is certainly plenty to see between the Rhine and Andermatt, the old pass village at the northern end of the St Gotthard. It's almost impossible to hurry, and anyone deciding on a detour – to the Rigi or the picturesque Stein am Rhein – should plan on an overnight stay.

SCHAFFHAUSEN

If the Rhine were ever to be considered the natural northern border of Switzerland, then ★ **Schaffhausen** (pop. 34,000) would definitely end up on the wrong side of it. The Rhine Falls (Rheinfall) have always formed a natural geographical obstacle to river traffic, forcing ships to unload their cargoes, and this soon led to the region being settled. Schaffhausen became a free imperial city in the 13th century, and in 1501 it joined the Swiss Confederation to protect itself against the Habsburgs.

The mighty, cylindrical 16th-century fort known as the ★ **Munot** towers above this town which, though industrial, has retained much of its former splendour.

The centre of town is the **Fronwagplatz** with its fountains, and the three most attractive streets in Schaffhausen lead away from here: the short Oberstadt goes westwards to the 13th-century Obertor; Vorstadt, with its many oriel-windowed townhouses, leads northwards; and Vordergasse runs off to the east, with the 15th-century Rathaus on the right and the Haus zum Ritter. The famous ★ **painted façade** of the latter was the work of Tobias Stimmer (1568–70).

The Rhine Falls

To the south of Vordergasse, on the Münster-platz, is the Romanesque ★ **Münster**; built around 1100, it is a pillared basilica with a transept and five-storey bell-tower. Before the Reformation, this Protestant municipal church belonged to a Benedictine monastery.

The monastic dependencies next to it today house the **Allerheiligen Museum** (Tuesday to Sunday 10am–noon and 2–5pm); its varied exhibits include several prehistoric finds, some contemporary art, and a valuable piece of ★ **onyx** captured by the Swiss from the Burgundian arch-duke Charles the Bold in 1476, at the Battle of Grandson (*see pages 17 and 73*).

THE RHINE FALLS AND STEIN AM RHEIN

A detour to the nearby ★★ **Rhine Falls** (Rheinfall) is strongly recommended at this point. Near Neuhausen the cataract is 150m (490ft) wide and thunders down from a 20-m (65-ft) high limestone cliff – a grandiose sight, especially during June and July when the river is swollen by snow melt. The best view of the rapids is from the 12th-century Schlösschen Wörth, and for a close-up, try the observation points on the left bank. The small island in the middle can be reached by taking the launch.

From Schaffhausen there's a good excursion by boat to ★ **Stein am Rhein** (pop. 2,600), just

Star Attraction
• Rhine Falls

Below: the Munot
Bottom: Stein am Rhein

Below: tile details, St Georgen
Bottom: Cranach's Portrait of
Dr. Johannes Cuspinian

20km (12 miles) further upriver. Its fortified towers, well-preserved fortress, painted façades and houses with oriel windows – especially near the Rathausplatz – all combine to create a largely intact medieval market town.

Right next to the river is the Benedictine abbey of **St Georgen** (open Mar–Nov: Tues–Sun 9am–noon and 1.30–5pm); the church, a pillared basilica, dates from the Romanesque period. Its late medieval section is now a museum and conveys a good impression of what monastic life during the Middle Ages must have been like.

WINTERTHUR

Winterthur (pop. 89,000) had its origins in the Gallo-Roman camp of Vitudurum, but was refounded in 1170 by the counts of Kyburg. For centuries the town was dwarfed by Zürich, and was even sold to it in 1467, since when it has been in a state of permanent rivalry with its powerful neighbour. With the advent of industrialisation in the 19th century and the disappearance of protectionist trade barriers, Winterthur rapidly became an important industrial centre. It began with the textile industry, which led to the textile machine industry and further diversification into turbines, engines and locomotives.

The town has several magnificent art collections dating back to the years of industrial expansion. The **Kunstmuseum** (open Tues10am–8pm, Wed–Sun 10am–5pm) contains works by many fine artists, from Renoir to Picasso. Even more of an eye-opener is the ★ **Oskar Reinhart Collection** (open Tues–Sun 10am–5pm) at Am Römerholz on the north side of Stadthausstrasse. French 19th-century painters are joined here by priceless old masters, including pictures by Brueghel, Rubens, Rembrandt, El Greco and Goya.

The scientifically-minded will enjoy a visit to the ★★ **Technorama** (open Tues–Sun 10am–5pm) in Frauenfelder Strasse, Oberwinterthur, a fascinating and enormous exhibition of the technical history of Switzerland from the early 19th century to the present.

Map on pages 44–5

ZUG

The route now continues via Zürich *(see page 39)* to ★ **Zug** (pop. 24,000). This friendly town, capital of the tiny canton of the same name, lies on the northeastern shore of the Zugersee (38sq km/14sq miles). From the promenade there's a good view of the Pilatus and the Rigi, and between them, on clear days, it's even possible to make out the distant peaks of the Bernese Alps.

At the centre of the old town is the picturesque Kolinplatz with Zug's symbol, the **Zytturm** (1480) with its astronomical clock. It is one of four medieval gates that survive from the fortifications. The 11th-century Burg contains the **Historical Museum** (open Tues–Fri 2–5pm, Sat–Sun 10am–noon, 2–5pm), with displays on the region's cultural history.

The little town of **Goldau** (pop. 4,700) lies between two famous mountains, ★ **Rigi** and **Rossberg** (1,580m/5,180ft). The latter was the scene of the worst accident in Swiss history: in September 1806, after heavy rains, a landslide destroyed Goldau and surrounding villages, killing over 500 people. From the summit of Rossberg, the extent of the catastrophe can still be visualised.

Further along the route there is an excellent view from the Bernrhöhe (555m/1,820ft) up to the weird-looking symmetrical rocky peaks known as

Star Attraction
• Technorama

Delightful old town
Winterthur's old quarter is a reminder of the town's prosperous 19th century. Marktgasse, with late Gothic and baroque townhouses, has been turned into a lively pedestrian shopping area.

The Zytturm

Map
on pages
44–5

The richest place in Switzerland

The tiny canton of Zug has the lowest tax rates in Switzerland (about half the average) which has attracted thousands of multinational corporations and raised the per capita annual income to about 70,000 Swiss francs.

The Rathaus, Schwyz

the Mythen (1,899m/6,230ft). At their foot lies ★ **Schwyz** (pop. 13,000), the town to which the Swiss owe the name of their country and their national coat-of-arms. There are a number of impressive buildings here, of architectural interest; the **Ital-Reding-Haus**, for instance, with its two little domed towers. The man it was named after made his fortune as a mercenary, like so many inhabitants of the Forest Cantons; many never made it home, however, but died 'heroic deaths' while fighting for foreign lords.

At the centre of Schwyz is its cobbled main square, with the attractive, frescoed **Rathaus** (1645). Not too far out of town, on the road towards Seewen, is the **Bundesbriefarchiv** (Swiss Federal Archives; open daily 9–11.30am, 2–5pm), a frequent excursion for Swiss schoolchildren. This is where important documents relating to the foundation and history of the old Confederation are stored – including the *Bundesbrief* of 1291.

Brunnen (pop. 7,500) lies at the mouth of the Muota; from its lakeside promenade there is a good view of the enormous Schillerstein on the opposite shore. This isolated crag was inscribed in honour of the German poet and dramatist, Friedrich von Schiller, who wrote *William Tell* in 1804, and was mainly responsible for the Tell legend. Interestingly enough, Schiller never once visited the Alps. Very close by is the **Rütli Meadow**, the sacred site of the solemn, eternal oath sworn by the men of Uri, Schwyz and Unterwalden in 1291 *(see page 16)*.

MOUNTAIN PASSES

The famous ★ **Axenstrasse** connects Brunnen with Flüelen. Opened in 1865, it runs along the rocky eastern bank of the Urner See and is one of the most picturesque sections of road in Switzerland, offering stunning views at every turn. In **Altdorf**, in the Uri canton, *William Tell* is performed once every three years by amateur actors at the Tellspielhaus (performances are scheduled for 2004, 2007 and 2010).

In **Wassen** (pop. 600) the magnificent ★ **Susten Pass-Strasse** branches off to the right; it connects the Reuss Valley with the Berner Haslital, and is part of the famous ★ **Three Passes Route** via ★★ **Susten** (2,224m/7,300ft), ★★ **Grimsel** (2,165m/7,100ft) and ★ **Furka** (2,431m/7,970ft), providing unforgettable views of the spectacular mountain landscape.

Star Attractions
•**Susten**
•**Grimsel**

SCHÖLLENEN RAVINE TO ANDERMATT

The small town of **Göschenen** lies right next to the northern entrance of both Gotthard tunnels: the railway tunnel, 15km (9 miles) long and now more than 100 years old, and the new road tunnel that was opened in 1980 (16km/10 miles). Above the village the valley narrows to form the wild ★ **Schöllenen Ravine**, which only became accessible from the 13th century onwards. Crossing the famous Teufelsbrücke over the wild Reuss river is an impressive experience.

Below: a Susten Pass view
Bottom: the Schöllenen Ravine

Andermatt (pop. 1,600), where this route ends, is a popular winter sports resort at the heart of the Swiss Alps. From here there are pass routes leading south over the St Gotthard Pass and into the Ticino *(see page 52)*, westward over the Furka to Valais *(see page 95)* and eastwards across the Oberalp (2,044m/6,700ft) to the valley of the Upper Rhine.

Map
on pages
44–5

Ticino wine
A hundred years ago, the vineyards of Ticino were destroyed by the phylloxera louse. In 1905, Merlot vines were brought from Bordeaux to replace those lost. They thrived in their new home and today 85 percent of the 900 hectares (2,220 acres) of vineyards are covered by Merlot vines, producing about 4 million litres (20 million gallons) of Ticino wine annually.

Map of the St Gotthard Pass

7: Switzerland's Sunny South

Andermatt – St Gotthard Pass – Bellinzona – Lugano – Chiasso (136km/84 miles)

Ticino is one of the most popular regions of Switzerland, and is also the sunniest. The lakes and mountains and the Mediterranean climate attract visitors all year round, and the holiday centres, beaches and campsites can get quite crowded. There's another Ticino, however: the high valleys of the Sopra Ceneri are far from prosperous, and the picturesque façades hide the realities of decay, poverty and depopulation. It is contrasts like these that make the region so fascinating, however – especially on the journey from Lago di Maggiore into the Maggia or Verzasca valleys. Remember to allow for at least one night's stay.

THE LEVENTINA

From Andermatt *(see page 51)* it is only another 12km (7 miles) to the **St Gotthard Pass** (2,108m/6,916ft). The stark beauty of this region is typical of the Central Alps. The trip down the other side affords magnificent views of the Bedretto Valley and of the **Leventina** – the name given to the section of the Ticino valley between Airolo and Biasca. In Biasca, you can stop to admire the delightful frescoes in the church of San Pietro.

Although the sharp increase in road traffic and the ensuing pollution is giving it trouble, the Leventina still has some very attractive landscapes. Higher up, there are still picturesque corners and quiet valleys, and old houses here and there still look very much the way they always have.

In **Giornico**, make a detour to the 11th-century ★ **Church of San Nicolao**. This granite building with its atmospheric interior is considered the finest Romanesque structure in Ticino.

BELLINZONA, CAPITAL OF TICINO

Because of its strategically favourable location near the main Alpine passes, **Bellinzona** (pop.

18,000), the capital of Ticino, was fought over many times by the Milanese nobility and the Confederation. The Swiss finally managed to gain lasting control of it at the beginning of the 16th century. No wonder the town is still famous for its medieval ★ **fortifications**: high above the Lombard-style Città is the 12th-century **Castello Grande**, and to the east the 13th-century **Castello Montebello** is one of the finest castles in Switzerland. The fortress high up on the mountain slope is the **Castello di Sasso Corbaro** (1479). All three of these castles contain regional museums.

DETOUR TO LAKE MAGGIORE

★★ **Locarno** (pop. 18,500), 20km (12 miles) from Bellinzona, is the second most important tourist centre in Ticino after Lugano *(see page 54)*. The mild climate and delightful landscape have attracted Northern Europeans here for decades. It was only after World War II, however, that the tourist boom really began and spread to include the neighbouring municipalities of Muralto, Minusio, Orselina and Brione.

Despite recent developments, particularly in the service sector, this town on the northern shore of **Lago di Maggiore** has retained its charm, a successful mixture of rural-Alpine on the one hand and Mediterranean on the other. At the centre of

Star Attraction
• Locarno

Below: a San Nicolao fresco
Bottom: Bellinzola's
Castello Grande

Map
on pages
44–5

Locarno is the long Piazza Grande, where the annual film festival is held in August; there's also a weekly market (open Thur 8am–noon). This square can get pretty crowded, but the streets in the old part of town just beyond are far quieter.

At the southwestern corner of the **Città Vecchia** is the Castell, which is all that remains today of the once-mighty Visconti Fortress, most of which was razed to the ground by the Confederation in 1532. High on a rocky outcrop above the town is the 17th-century pilgrimage church of **Madonna del Sasso**, which is also a good place to admire the view.

The Centovalli Railway Take the little clanky train from Locarno and discover one of the country's most scenic rides, as it winds slowly over the 'hundred valleys' from which it gets its name, on rickety bridges and aqueducts.

The lakeside in Ascona

ASCONA

★ **Ascona** (pop. 5,000) is only 3km (1½ miles) away from Locarno. At the turn of the 20th century it was still a sleepy lakeside village, before it became popular with artists, naturists and aristocrats. Today, Ascona is a cosmopolitan holiday resort; beyond its broad, lakeside promenade, lined with cafés, are the narrow streets of the Borgo, or old town. Buildings of particular interest include the Casa Borrani, with an early baroque façade (1620), the cloister of the Collegio Papio, and the church of **Santa Maria della Misericordia** with fine 15th-century frescoes.

To get to know this part of Switzerland properly, take a detour into the remote valleys of the Sopra Ceneri. The ★ **Val Verzasca** near Gordola has some magnificent rocky scenery; and ★ **Corippo**, 9km (5 miles) from Gordola, is considered the best-kept mountain village in Ticino. Sotto Ceneri is hillier than Sopra Ceneri, and has a Mediterranean feel to it. **Monte Ceneri** (554m/ 1,800ft) separates the two.

LUGANO

★★ **Lugano** (pop. 29,000), the largest town in Ticino, lies in a semi-circular bay on Lago di Lugano, between the mountains of Monte Brè and San Salvatore. This picturesque backdrop made it a popular holiday destination back in the very earliest days of tourism. Its warm weather (Lugano gets around 2,000 hours of sunshine a year) and subtropical vegetation give the city a real Mediterranean flair. The inroads of modern tourism have left their mark, however, and the city centre is now partially closed to cars, to reduce pollution and prevent overcrowding.

The town has several very attractive arcaded streets, such as the Via Pessina and the Via Nassa. The **Cathedral of San Lorenzo** towers above the tiled roofs of the town; its ★ **façade** (1500–17) is regarded as one of the best examples of early Renaissance architecture in Ticino. The monumental fresco of the *Passion* (Bernardino Luini, 1529) in the church of **Santa Maria degli Angeli** at the southern end of the Via Nassa, is also quite remarkable.

LAKESIDE ART

To the east of the old town, the leafy Parco Civico is an oasis of peace and tranquillity in comparison with the busy quaysides. In the park you will find the **Villa Ciani**, which houses the **Municipal Art Museum** (open Tues–Sun 10am–noon and 2–6pm). Close by, in Via Canova, is the **Museo Cantonale d'Arte** (open Tues 2–6pm, Wed–Sun 10am–5pm), containing several impressive works by Ticino artists.

Star Attraction
• Lugano

Below: Madonna del Sasso
Bottom: Piazza del Riforma, Lugano

Map
on pages
44–5

Below: Villa Favorita
Bottom: Lago di Lugano

Even though most of the famous Thyssen-Bornemisza collection has now been moved to Madrid (and part of it to Barcelona), it's still worth visiting the ★ **Villa Favorita** (open 10 April–1 Nov: Fri–Sun 10am–6pm) in Castagnola. The museum in this late 17th-century villa was reopened in 1993 and now contains works by 19th- and 20th-century American and European artists. It also holds numerous interesting temporary exhibitions.

In recent years, Ticino has become known as a centre of finance and services, as well as architecture. In 1996 the first Italian-language Swiss university was founded in Lugano.

LAKE LUGANO

Three quarters of ★★ **Lago di Lugano** (Lake Lugano; 48sq km/18sq miles) belongs to Switzerland. As with Lake Luzern, the *Ceresio*, as it is known to local people, is made up of several smaller lakes. Though the scenery is not as spectacular as in Luzern, there are fine views across the lake from Lugano's peaks, Monte Brè (925m/3,034ft) and San Salvatore (912m/2,992ft), both of which can only be reached by cable car. The best way to appreciate the lake, however, is from a boat. All the pleasure craft visit the picturesque fishing village of ★ **Gandria**, over on the eastern shore.

MELIDE AND MORCOTE

The small town of **Melide** (pop. 1,400) has a special attraction in store: the famous **Swissminiatur**, a model village showing Switzerland's best-known sights in miniature.

Just 5km (3 miles) further southwest is ★★**Morcote** (pop. 700), dominated by its 15th-century church of **Santa Maria del Sasso**, which is reached by climbing a flight of 406 steps. This architectural ensemble is still intact, and has been spared the adverse effects of property speculation. Tourism here continues to increase, however, and this tiny village can get extremely crowded in peak season.

THE GOLDEN HILL

To the southwest of Lugano is **Collina d'Oro**, or 'Golden Hill', which makes an ideal excursion from Lugano (via Agra). The cemetery of the 16th-century church of **San Abbondio** here contains the grave of the German poet, novelist and philosopher, Hermann Hesse (1877–1962), who spent much of his life in Ticino.

Capolago (pop. 600) lies at the southern end of Lago di Lugano. If you are interested in seeing a fantastic view you should take the rack railway from here up to the summit of **Monte Generoso** (1,701m/5,581ft).

For some magnificent architecture you should visit the neighbouring village of **Riva San Vitale**, with the domed church of ★**Santa Croce** (1588–92) and its ★baptistery (c. 500); the latter is a fascinating relic of the Early Christian era.

TOWARDS THE ITALIAN BORDER

Mendrisio (pop. 7,000) is the capital of the Mendrisiotto; it's a bit industrial now, but the old town centre contains several worthwhile places to see. The rolling hills around the town are ideal for excursions; one favourite destination is the ★**Valle di Muggio**, with its tiny, pretty villages. The route finally arrives at the Italian border near **Chiasso** (pop. 8,500).

Star Attractions
• Lake Lugano
• Morcote

The grottoes
Nothing is more typical of life in Ticino than the grottoes, simple taverns in quiet, hidden away places, shaded by trees. They are set in generous gardens with solid granite tables and benches, where guests can enjoy the local cuisine: home-made, air-dried sausages, minestrone, risotto, marinated fish, vitello tonnato, polenta, roast beef, rabbit stew, cheese and local wines, or *Barbera con la gazzosa*, a local lemon soda.

Gandria from the lake

Map
on pages
44–5

8: Lakes, Glaciers and Ravines: over the San Bernardino

St Gallen – Vaduz – Chur – Passo del San Bernardino – Bellinzona (231km/143 miles)

The San Bernardino Pass is the most important north–south route after the Gotthard, and is open all year, thanks to its tunnel. It connects three important regions of Switzerland: the Bodensee area, Grisons and Ticino. This results in a mix of landscapes and impressions ranging from the cheerful to the dramatic: fruit trees and vines in the Rhine Valley; wild ravines in the Lower Rhine; ice and snow up on the San Bernadino itself; and then, in Misox, a whiff of the Mediterranean. Those intending to make detours to the Grisons Oberland or to Arosa should plan on an overnight stay.

ST GALLEN

St Gallen (pop. 72,000), capital of the canton, lies in the foothills of the Appenzeller Mountains. It is named after the Irish monk Gallus, who settled here in 612. His retreat became the abbey which, between the 9th and 11th centuries, was one of the most important spiritual centres in Europe. The magnificent baroque ★★ **Stiftskirche** (1755–66) testifies to that former glory.

St Gallen embroidery
Embroidery has a long history in St Gallen, as it was already being made for export in the 18th century. The invention in the early 19th century of machines that could do the work was the beginning of a golden age for the city. By 1913, embroidery was Switzerland's largest export, and St Gallen produced half the world's embroidered textiles. Today it is only .05 percent but it is still considered desirable because of its high quality.

The Stiftsbibliothek, St Gallen

The main attraction here, however, is the ★★★**Stiftsbibliothek** (Abbey Library; open May–Oct: Mon–Sat 9am–noon, 2–5pm, Sun 10.30am–noon and July–Aug: also 2–4pm; Nov–April: Tues–Sat 9am–noon and 2–4pm). This library hall (1763) is a masterpiece of rococo architecture, and contains many treasures, such as the Carolingian plan of the abbey (AD 820) or the 8th-century Irish gospels.

DETOUR TO APPENZELL

Appenzell, one of the smallest cantons in Switzerland, is composed of two demicantons, Inner-Rhoden and Ausser-Rhoden. The cheese from this region is world famous. Here, at the foot of the Säntis, the villages with their typical Appenzeller houses contrast attractively with the green meadows and the grey of the Alpine massif higher up. A good way of exploring Appenzell is to take the train from St Gallen.

Near Buchs, the small town of ★ **Werdenberg** has several houses dating from the late Middle Ages, and a 15th-century castle. Werdenberg has the oldest and best-preserved collection of wooden buildings in Switzerland.

On the other side of the Rhine, at the foot of the **Three Sisters** (2,052m/6,732ft), lies **Vaduz** (pop. 5,000), capital of the principality of Liechtenstein. The small town is dominated by a castle, the residence of the royal family. **Liechtenstein** (pop. 30,000) covers an area of just 160sq km (62sq miles) and originated when the Lordship of Schellenberg and County of Vaduz merged in 1719.

CHUR

It's clear from any map that the town of ★ **Chur** (pop. 33,000) is the strategic gateway to the mountainous region of Grisons. The first settlement here dates back to the Stone Age. Roman generals, German emperors, prince-bishops, the Habsburgs and the French all tried to gain control of this important route through to Italy at some time or another.

Star Attraction
• **St Gallen Monastery**

Below: St Gallen's Textile Museum
Bottom: Appenzell glass

Map on pages 44–5

Below: the Gothic altar, Chur cathedral
Bottom: the Martinskirche ceiling

Towering above the tiny streets is the mighty complex created by the Episcopal Court and the ★ **Cathedral** – an important late Romanesque structure with magnificent sculpture and a fine interior; highlights include the marble slabs on the Carolingian altar to St Lawrence and the ★ **Gothic altar** by Jakob Russ (1492). The treasure in the **Cathedral Museum** (open Mon–Fri 3.30–5pm) is definitely worth a visit; there are several early medieval artefacts on display. Other sights in Chur include the **Rathaus**, which dates from 1494 and has a very fine Renaissance panelled chamber (1583); and several attractive old townhouses in Kirchgasse.

EXCURSIONS FROM CHUR

To the east of Chur, road and railway wind their way through the deep valley of the Plessur for 29km (18 miles) to the mountain health resort of ★ **Arosa** (pop. 2,600).

A 20-km (12-mile) drive to the west of Chur is another famous holiday resort, ★ **Flims** (pop. 2,600), renowned for its Weisse Arena skiing region between Vorab and Flimserstein. The village lies close to the ★ **Rhine Ravine** (Ruinaulta), the largest in the country.

Some 60km (37 miles) from Chur, the village of **Disentis**, with a fine ★ **baroque church**, sits at the confluence of the Medelser and the Upper Rhine. Two pass routes begin here: the first is to the west, where the road and the railway climb to the **Oberalp** (2,044m/6,706ft); the second is a modern section of road heading south through the barren Val Medels and up to the **Lukmanier** (1,916m/6,286ft). After Lukmanier the road descends into the ★ **Val Blenio** – an interesting alternative to the much-used San Bernardino route (Chur–Disentis–Biasca, 120km/75 miles).

Continuing towards the San Bernardino, the valley of the Rhine suddenly narrows to form a gorge, the ★★ **Via Mala**. You can walk to the gorge from Sils im Domleschg along a new path the **Kulturweg** (1½ hours; for information, contact the Thusis Tourist Office, tel: 081- 651 1134

Driving along the recently-built N3 it's hard to imagine the gorge was once dangerous – but from the old cantonal road (the car park with a kiosk just after the first bridge) there's a flight of steps leading down into its foaming depths. At the end of the Via Mala in **Zillis**, break your journey briefly to visit the 12th-century **Martinskirche**. Its choir dates from 1509; and its renowned ★★★ **wooden ceiling**, with 153 panels relating the *Life of Christ*, from around 1160.

Star Attractions
•Via Mala
•Martinskirche
wooden ceiling

SAN BERNARDINO WATERSHED

Near the village of **Splügen** the road (inaugurated in 1822) comes out above the Splügen Pass. The old cantonal road then winds its way up as far as the **Passo del San Bernardino** (2,065m/ 6,775ft), the watershed between the Rhine and the Po.

Near **Mesocco** (pop. 1,100) the first chestnut trees appear, heralding a change in climate. The Misox, or Val Mesolcina, is one of three Italian-speaking valleys in Grisons. In medieval times this region was ruled by the lords of Sax-Misox; the ruin of their fortress lies on a rocky rise above the River Moésa, between Mesocco and Soazza.

After passing through Roveredo the route crosses the border of Ticino, and ends in **Bellinzona** *(see page 53)*.

Liechtenstein
Since 1924 this tiny state (the world's fourth smallest) has had a customs treaty with Switzerland. It has the Swiss franc as its currency, but produces its own collectable stamps, and the Engländerbau next to the post office in Vaduz houses the Stamp Museum. Next door is the impressive State Art Collection (daily 10am–noon, 1.30–5.30pm).

The Passo del San Bernardino

Map
on pages
44–5

Below: Langenbruck castle
Bottom: a Liestal façade

9: Across the Linguistic Divide

Basel – Bern – Fribourg – Montreux – Col du Grand St-Bernard (292km/181 miles)

This route leads through the three main landscapes of Switzerland: the Jura near Basel, the Mittelland and then the high mountains. It starts at the famous bend in the Rhine in Basel and ends up at the top of the highest mountains in the Valais Alps. There are several magnificent towns to visit along the way, such as Solothurn, Murten and Fribourg, and numerous castles bear witness to the turbulent history of this region along the German-Swiss and French-Swiss border. This route can be done in a day, but that would be a real shame.

SOLOTHURN

Liestal (pop. 13,000), the capital of the canton of Basel-Land, is just 15km (9 miles) from Basel itself, having split off from it in 1833. Drive from here via Waldenberg and up to the **Obere Hauenstein** (738m/2,401ft), an ancient Jura pass that was regularly used by the Romans. **Langenbruck**, just after the top of the pass, is an ideal starting-point for hikes through the region. One of the walks leads to the 4-km (2-mile) distant **Belchenfluh** (1,123m/3,684ft); there's a magnificent Alpine panorama from the top.

The region around ★ ★ **Solothurn** (pop. 16,000) was first settled during the Mesolithic period. A 17th-century chronicler named Franz Haffner claimed that Solothurn had been founded '1,276 years before the powerful city of Rome', but that is an exaggeration to say the least. Evidence does exist, however, of a Roman settlement called *Salodurum*.

Traditional life and architecture are cherished here, and the old part of Solothurn, with pretty little houses and medieval fortifications, is very atmospheric. From 1530 to 1792 the town was the residence of the French envoy to the Confederation, and some of this 'Valais' past still survives today: local people may speak German, but they feel far more French.

HISTORIC CENTRE

The symbol of the city is ★ **St Ursen Cathedral** (1762–73), an early Swiss-neoclassical structure which, despite its enormous dimensions, blends in very well with the old town. Several more buildings in the town centre are worthy of note: the 12th-century **Zeitglockenturm**, with its astronomical clock added in the 16th century, is one; the ★ **Jesuit Church** (1680–89), which contains some fine stucco by Ticino artists, is another; and there is the Rathaus (Town Hall), originally Gothic but much extended in the 17th century. The free-standing Arsenal (Zeughaus), built between 1610 and 1614, is also impressive; today it houses a fascinating arms collection.

Less military is the **Historical Museum** (open Wed–Sat 2–5pm, Sun 10am–noon, 2–5pm) in Schloss Blumenstein, which includes an interesting and informative exhibition on life in Solothurn during the 18th century. The **Art Museum** (open Tues–Sat 10am–noon, 2–5pm, Sun 10am–5pm) mostly contains works by 19th- and 20th-century Swiss artists.

A VISIT TO THE EMMENTAL

Further on towards Bern, a rewarding detour – and not only for cheese lovers – can be made to the ★ **Emmental**. This hilly region on either side

Star Attraction
• Solothurn

Solothurn's old town
The baroque old town, first developed by the French ambassadors living there, is today a lively, cosmopolitan place, with a thriving industry (watch-making and precision manufacturing) and an interesting ethnic mix.

The Jesuit Church organ, Solothurn

Map on pages 44–5

Chilbi

Chilbi is the generic term for the summer highland festivals of the Emmental, with folk singers and dancers, yodellers, flag-throwers, alphorn blowers, and – in August – the *Lüderenchilbi*, traditional Swiss wrestling.

Making cheese in Emmenthal

of the Emme River, with its green meadows and pretty farmhouses, is like something straight from a picture postcard. At the entrance to the valley is the town of **Burgdorf** (pop. 15,500), dominated by its mighty 12th-century castle, once the seat of the Bernese *landvogts*. Today it houses the Folklore Museum.

MURTEN

Go via the country's capital of Bern *(see page 25)* now to reach ★ **Murten** (pop. 4,600) on the frontier of the German-speaking region. This town lies on a small rise on the southeastern shore of a lake of the same name. The small, walled town with its castle appears to have changed little since medieval times. Murten is famous for an important event in Swiss history: the Confederation's second and decisive defeat of the Burgundian archduke, Charles the Bold, in 1476. The view down the main street with its baroque houses, towards the 18th-century Berntor gate, is particularly attractive.

FRIBOURG

★★★ **Fribourg** (pop. 35,000) capital of the mainly French-speaking canton of the same name, was founded by Berchtold IV of Zähringen in 1157. Historically, it has always stood in the shadow of Bern, its larger neighbour, and despite the odd alliance the two towns never got on very well with each other – not even after Fribourg joined the Confederation in 1481. There is a particularly impressive view of the historic town centre and its fortifications from the Zähringer Brücke.

GOTHIC SPLENDOUR

The monumental Gothic ★ **Cathedral of St Nicholas** dominates the ensemble. It was built between 1283 and 1490; the side-chapels came later, and the Gothic-style choir was added as late as 1631. A spiral staircase leads to the top o the 76-m (249-ft) tower. This three-aisled basilica contains several sculptural masterpieces, including a fine ★ *Entombment* dating from 1433, a choir screen from 1466, and some beautiful art nouveau, stained-glass windows by Jozef Mehoffer. The church organ was played by Franz Liszt, among others.

The walled settlement of Fribourg began to spread across the natural defensive site of the Saane Peninsula as early as the 13th century. The Bourg quarter and the Auge quarter of town have both retained their medieval appearance and are ideal places to wander around. At the western end of the oldest part of the town is the Rathaus, a late Gothic building with an octagonal clock-tower and oriel windows.

NINE CENTURIES OF ART

Not far away is the **Franciscan Church**, the Eglise des Cordéliers. It contains one very fine work of art, an ★ *Altarpiece of the Crucifixion*, an important 15th-century work by the Master of the Carnation. The choir stalls, dating from 1280, are among the oldest in the country.

From the church it's only a short walk to the Villa Ratzé, an elegant Renaissance building dating from 1585. Here art from nine centuries can be admired in the **Musée d'Art et d'Histoire**

Star Attraction
•Fribourg

Below: from Fribourg's Eglise des Cordéliers
Bottom: a view of Fribourg

Map
on pages
44–5

(open Tues–Sun 10am–5pm, Thur also 8–10pm) and the **Espace Jean Tinguely–Niki de Saint Phalle** displays work by the well-known Fribourg artist (open Wed–Sun 10am–5pm, Thur also 8–10pm).

EXCURSIONS FROM FRIBOURG

Among interesting sights in the immediate vicinity is the Roman town of **Avenches** (pop. 2,000), 14km (9 miles) from Fribourg, which was once the capital of Helvetia with a population 10 times its present one. An amphitheatre and long section of wall (open daily 9am–noon, 1–5pm) remain.

Also in the Vaud and 20km (12 miles) to the west is **Payerne** (pop. 7,000). Its former ★ **abbey church** (10th–12th century) has a bright, albeit austere, interior and is one of the most important Romanesque buildings in Switzerland.

> **Gruyères**
> In this perfectly preserved old town, where cars are banned but not tourists, almost every dish on the menu of every restaurant includes the famous cheese, or the local, butterfat-rich double cream. Walking to and from the village is good for the legs and the digestion.

Cheese in storage, Gruyère

GRUYERES

A short distance south of Fribourg, on a bend in the River Saane at the entrance to the ★ **Gruyère** region, lies **Hauterive Abbey**, founded in 1138. Its ★ **church** is a typical example of 12th-century Cistercian architecture, and it has a fine cloister.

The word *Gruyère* usually brings cheese to people's minds, and the secrets of how the famous cheese is produced are divulged at the Schaukäserei at **Pringy**, a short distance outside the town of **Gruyères**.

After this ancient hill town, there are several more places of interest to see in the region, including **Bulle** (pop. 8,500), with an impressive 13th-century castle. The **Musée Gruérien** (open Tues–Sat 10am–noon, 2–5pm, Sun 2–5pm), containing collections documenting local history and culture, is also worth a look.

VEVEY

★ **Vevey** (pop. 16,000) is magnificently situated on the northern shore of Lac Léman. The famous vineyards of the Lavaux surround the busy town, which is the headquarters of the Swiss firm, Nestlé. It all began with milk: in 1867 Henri Nestlé (1814–90) began manufacturing powdered milk here, and in 1905 his firm merged with its main competitor, the Anglo-Swiss Condensed Milk Company. Chocolate soon became an important product, and eventually the company scored its greatest coup: Nescafé. Today Nestlé is one of the world's largest, and more controversial, companies. Its headquarters are housed in the huge, Y-shaped glass building in the town centre.

The main attractions in Vevey, however, are the delightful landscape and the excellent white wines. Both can be enjoyed at one of the observation points above the town: either **Mont Pèlerin** (810m/2,657ft; access via road and ropeway) or the **Pleiades** (1,360m/4,462ft; rack railway). Railway enthusiasts should combine a trip to the Pleiades with a visit to the Railway Museum (open May–Oct) in **Blonay**. The town also has an imposing 16th-century château, with a tower dating from 1175.

Star Attraction
•**Montreux**

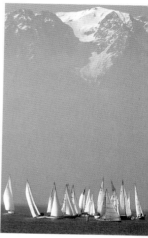

*Below: Mont Blance seen
from Montreux
Bottom: Montreux's hotel
Eden au Lac*

MONTREUX

A little further along the lake the route reaches ★★**Montreux** (pop. 20,000), centre of the famous 'Vaud Riviera' spa and holiday region. The town is a mixture of the old and the new: the modern

Map on pages 44–5

congress centre and casino contrast sharply with the palatial 19th-century hotels, which still retain much of their former splendour and elegance.

Another Belle Époque survivor is the rack railway leading up to the ★ **Rochers de Naye** (2,042m/6,700ft); at the top there's an Alpengarten and a magnificent panorama. Montreux is probably best known internationally for its vibrant **Jazz Festival**, held in July and August each year; visitors should reserve accommodation well in advance because it's a popular event.

CHILLON AND ST-MAURICE

The fairy-tale ★ **Castle of Chillon**, not far from Montreux, is situated on a rock overlooking the lake; some sections of it date from the 10th century. Bern took the castle in 1536 and freed the prior François Bonivard, who had been thrown into the dungeons six years earlier for supporting the Reformation in Geneva. This historical episode was later dramatised by Lord Byron in his poem *The Prisoner of Chillon* (1817).

Situated at the once-fortified entrance to the Valais, the largest valley in Switzerland *(see pages 95–9)*, is **St-Maurice** (pop. 3,500). According to legend it was here in around AD 300 that the 'warrior saint', St Maurice, was martyred along with his troops of the Theban Legion. In 515 the

Seeking peace in Caux
On the railway line up the mountain from Montreux to Rochers-de-Naye, you will find the turreted home of the Conference Centre for Moral Re-Armament, a collective that seeks to ease global political and economic strife through personal religious reconciliation, conferences and workshops.

The Castle of Chillon

Burgundian king Sigismond built a monastery here in his memory, and it remained a bastion of Christianity for centuries. The Abbey of St-Maurice is the oldest in Switzerland; some unique works from antiquity and the Middle Ages can be admired in the ★ **treasury**.

MARTIGNY

Martigny (pop. 14,000) lies on the 'elbow' of the Rhône valley, not far from the mouth of the Drance. As a town it is uninteresting, but it is worth a visit because of the ★ **Fondation Pierre Gianadda** (open June–Oct: daily 9am–7pm; Feb–May: daily 10am–6pm; Nov–June: daily 10am–noon, 1.30–6pm). Here there is a small museum with excellent changing exhibits in a setting that includes Roman ruins, a sculpture garden and café, a beautiful view and an enjoyable automobile museum.

Martigny is strategically placed at the junction of several pass routes. One of the passes leads over the Col de la Forclaz (1,527m/5,010ft) to Chamonix, and the other leads to the ★ **Col du Grand St-Bernard** (2,469m/8,100ft), which connects Valais with the Aosta Valley in Italy. This pass is open in winter thanks to the 6-km (3¾-mile) long tunnel, completed in 1964.

THE GRAND ST-BERNARD

The Grand St-Bernard is not only set in magnificent landscape, it is also steeped in history. This route was once taken by Celts and Romans, and during medieval times many German emperors came past here on their way to Rome. During the 11th century St Bernard of Menthon founded a hospice, which is still run by Augustinian monks today. It was they who bred the world-famous St Bernard dog. These animals, wearing the legendary barrels of alcohol around their necks, have saved the lives of many snowbound wayfarers over the centuries. The Hospice Museum contains several Roman finds as well as ancient documents relating to the history of the hospice.

Below: St-Maurice
Bottom: the Col du Grand St-Bernard

Map
on pages
44–5

Brocante

A special browser's delight is going to one of the many *brocante* markets that take place regularly throughout the year. Half-way in price and quality between flea markets and serious antique shows, they are a wonderful way to see old items of everyday life – from old country tools and hand-carved furniture to fine porcelain, silver, old linens, postcards, jewellery, swords, books, sculpture and paintings. With practice one can often find a bargain. Annual schedules are published and available at shows or in shops.

Delémont city gate

10: From the Rhine to Lake Geneva

Basel – Biel – Neuchâtel – Lausanne – Geneva (257km/159 miles)

This route from the Rhine to the Rhône leads across two of the three great Swiss landscapes: the Jura and the Mittelland. It runs through the ancient mountains, atmospheric and forbidding with their vast forests and deep ravines, and into the cheerful, western part of the Mittelland, where there are lots of lakes and open landscapes. This contrast, combined with numerous cultural and historical attractions, makes the route particularly satisfying. Don't try to do it all in a day – there's far too much to see.

THE JURA

The first stop after Basel *(see page 20)* on this route is **Delémont** (pop. 12,000), the capital of the canton of Jura. Its historic, almost rectangular centre is dominated by the imposing-looking baroque château, formerly the summer residence of the bishops of Basel.

Delémont is the ideal base for discovering the ★ **Jura** – by car, on foot or even on horseback. There's a very good route from here via Franches Montagnes, La Chaux-de-Fonds and Vue des Alpes to Neuchâtel; the total distance is almost 100km (60 miles).

That distance includes a detour on the way. This is to ★ **St-Ursanne** (pop. 900), a lovely village on the River Doubs with enchanting old houses and narrow streets. The **Stiftskirche**, a Romanesque basilica, has a magnificent sculpted portal reminiscent of the Gallusporte on the Münster in Basel.

Saignelégier (pop. 1,800) is the centre of the horse-breeding trade in Franches Montagnes; a horse fair is held here each year on the second weekend in August *(see page 109)*. This broad plateau south of the Doubs and close to the French border is ideal for hiking or biking holidays, and in winter for cross-country skiing.

WATCH-MAKING CAPITAL

La Chaux-de-Fonds (pop. 38,000), situated in a broad, high valley in the Neuchâtel Jura, is the 'watch-making capital' of Switzerland. It was rebuilt according to a grid plan after a great fire in 1794. The highlight for visitors here is the remarkable underground watch museum, the ★**Musée International d'Horlogerie** (open May–Oct: Tues–Sun 10am–noon, 2–5pm; Nov–April: Tues–Sun 2–5pm), containing over 3,000 exhibits on the theme of timekeeping. There is also an audiovisual show.

BIEL

Further on, ★ **Biel/Bienne** (pop. 53,000), the second largest town in the canton of Bern, is worth visiting not only for its attractive location at the northeastern end of the lake of the same name, but because the mixture of languages is really delightful, and there are a number of interesting things to see. The **Museum Schwab** (open Tues–Sun 10am–noon, 2–5pm) at Seevorstadt 50, is devoted to finds from several lake villages. Traces of the town's Roman past can be seen at the Petinesca Excavation Site on the road to Bern.

At the heart of the town's historic centre is the ★ **Ring**, a picturesque square with the attractive Vennerbrunnen (1546). On the square's south-

Below: Horology Museum exhibit
Bottom: St-Ursanne

Map on pages 44–5

eastern side, the late Gothic Stadtkirche (municipal church), has splendid 15th-century, stained-glass windows.

ROUSSEAU'S ISLAND

The region around Biel contains some fine landscapes and several interesting sights, such as **St Peter's Island**, which can be reached by boat, although it is really a peninsula rather than an island. Jean-Jacques Rousseau stayed here in 1765. The two small medieval towns of **La Neuveville** and ★ **Le Landeron** are also very attractive, as is the ★ **Chasseral** (1,607m/5,270ft), 17km (12 miles) from La Neuveville, which is widely admired for its Alpine panorama.

NEUCHATEL

★★ **Neuchâtel/Neuenburg** (pop. 34,000) lies on the northern shore of the **Lac de Neuchâtel** (216sq km/83sq miles), which is the largest inland lake that lies completely inside Swiss territory. On clear days the distant peaks of the Alps can be seen across its calm waters. This region is steeped in history. The earliest traces of human settlement date back to the Stone Age and early Iron Age (400–58BC). The finds are on display in the **Musée d'Archéologie** (open Tues–Sun 10am–5pm). During the Middle Ages this city was a Burgundian stronghold, before being captured by German and French nobles and later by the Prussians. It was only in 1857, half a century after it became the twenty-first canton of the Confederation, that Prussia finally gave it up.

CHATEAU AND COLLEGIATE CHURCH

The city centre is dominated by a mighty complex of buildings comprising the **Château** and the ★ **Collégiale** (collegiate church). The oldest sections of the château, formerly the residence of the counts of Neuchâtel, date from the late 12th century; the building has undergone a great deal of alteration since then, however.

Sounds of yesteryear
The guided tour of the CIMA museum of music boxes, automata, singing birds and fairground instruments in Sainte-Croix offers visitors the delights of yesteryear's musical entertainments, and can be combined with a visit to the REUGE music box factory and other craftsmen's shops (open Tues–Sun 1.30–6pm); www.cima.ste-croix@bluewin.ch

Neuchâtel's Collégiale

The collegiate church, originally a three-aisled, 12th-century pillared basilica, has also changed greatly in appearance over the centuries. Inside, it contains a special treasure, the highly unusual Gothic ★ **Cenotaph of the Counts**, with 15 painted, life-sized effigies. They were created between 1372 and 1478, and the monument was restored during the 18th century.

A short walk to the west of the Château will take you to the interesting **Ethnographical Museum** (open Tues–Sun 10am–5pm) with extensive collections of cultural artefacts, primarily from Africa, Oceania and Asia.

The old part of Neuchâtel is clustered at the foot of the Château. At its centre is the **Place des Halles**; note the attractive oriel windows on the Maison des Halles (1570). The harbour-side quays are a good place for a walk; not far away is the **Musée d'Art et d'Histoire** (open Tues–Sun 10am–5pm), containing works by Swiss artists of the 15th to 20th centuries, as well as a remarkable collection of clocks and machines.

Star Attraction
•Neuchâtel

Below: a Place des Halles oriel window
Bottom: Grandson castle

GRANDSON

It was near **Grandson** (pop. 1,200) on 2 March 1476 that the Confederate army won their first victory over the Burgundian archduke, Charles the Bold. The small town is dominated by its

Map
on pages
44–5

Pestalozzi's vision

Johann Heinrich Pestalozzi was a visionary educator who devoted his life to providing poor children with the chance of an education. This revolutionary idea of education for all was adopted by Victorian reformers in Britain and elsewhere as an essential part of an effective welfare policy. His belief that 'head, heart, and hand' all had to be trained had a great influence, first on the Swiss and then the German school systems.

mighty, five-towered baronial ★ **castle**, which dates from the 13th century. One section has been turned into a museum featuring a banqueting hall, veteran car collection and a weapons exhibition.

YVERDON-LES-BAINS

At the southwestern end of the Lac de Neuchâtel is the spa town of **Yverdon-les-Bains** (pop. 23,000), known to the Romans as Eburodunum. Its sulphurous thermal springs have recently been reactivated. The massive castle, built in 1260 under Pierre II of Savoy, is a good example of the square-built style of that period *(carré savoyard)*, so common in the west of Switzerland. Today it houses the **Musée du Viel Yverdon** (open June–Sept: Tues–Sun 10am–noon, 2–5pm; Oct–May: 2–5pm) with a wealth of prehistoric and Roman material on display. One tower of the castle contains a room devoted to the life and work of educationalist Heinrich Pestalozzi, who established a school here in 1806.

LAC DE JOUX

There are several more pleasant detours between here and Lac Léman. One rewarding trip is into the Vaud Jura. Travel 25km (15 miles) from Yverdon via Vallorbe to the **Lac de Joux**. The calm,

A local fresco

silent countryside here is ideal for relaxing and gentle hiking (rather than the exhausting uphill variety). The region has more than its share of cultural sights, too. The ★ Roman mosaics at **Orbe** are definitely worth a visit, and don't miss the ★★ **monastery church** in **Romainmôtier**, 7km (4 miles) southwest of Orbe. This is one of the most famous Romanesque structures in Switzerland; the church, monastery and surrounding landscape combine to form a special and lasting impression of harmony and tranquillity.

LAUSANNE

★★ **Lausanne** (pop. 128,000), built on a series of terraces above Lake Geneva, is the second most important cultural and industrial centre in French-speaking Switzerland (after Geneva). Surrounded by a pleasant, hilly landscape and vineyards producing delicious Vaud wines, the town has a cosmopolitan, French edge to it. Zürich, with all its virtues and sobriety and high finance, seems worlds away.

Historically, Lausanne was usually overshadowed by Geneva, its larger neighbour. It began as a Roman settlement (several finds have been made in the suburb of Vidy). In 539 it was a bishop's see, and in 1032 became part of the Holy Roman Empire. Bern conquered the Vaud in 1610, and Lausanne lost its political significance. In 1803, after the collapse of the old confederation, the Vaud became a Swiss canton.

At the very centre of Lausanne is the **Place St-François** with the Gothic church of the same name. The square can be reached quickly from the Bergstation on the Lausanne Metro which connects Ouchy with the town centre. This part of Lausanne has been far more agreeable since it was closed to motor traffic.

NOTRE-DAME CATHEDRAL

On the Place de Palud is the 17th-century Hôtel de Ville (Town Hall). The Escaliers du Marché, partially roofed over, lead up to ★★ **Notre-Dame**

Star Attractions
• Romainmôtier church
• Lausanne
• Notre-Dame Cathedral

Below: Romainmôtier
Bottom: Lausanne cathedral

Map on pages 44–5

Enjoying the lakeside
To make the most of the beautiful waterfront of Lac Léman (Lake Geneva), try walking, cycling or rollerblading along the lakeside path from Lausanne to Morges. Most of it is undisturbed by traffic.

The train to Ouchy

Cathedral, in the upper part of town. Consecrated in 1275 after a century of construction, it is widely regarded as the finest example of Gothic architecture in Switzerland, and on a par with its counterparts in France. The sculpturally decorative Montfalcon Portal on the western façade was added in the early 16th century, in contrast to the far older Painted Portal. Inside is the striking ★ **rose window** in the south transept.

Below the cathedral is the broad Place de la Riponne, bordered at its eastern end by the **Palais de Rumine** (open daily 10am–noon, 2–5pm) with remarkable collections covering geology, zoology, history and archaeology. the building also houses an **Art Museum** (open Tues and Wed 11am–6pm, Thur 11am–8pm, Fri–Sun 11am–5pm), displaying works by artists from all over the region.

INSPIRING ART AND OLYMPIC FACTS

Unusual, but fascinating is the ★ **Collection de l'Art Brut** in the **Château de Beaulieu** (open Tues–Sun 11am–1pm, 2–6pm). The exhibits here are the work of patients from mental-health institutions, and other marginalised people. Much of the work is bizarre and disturbing, but nearly all of it is memorable, and often inspiring.

Down by the lake, not far from Lausanne's cosmopolitan suburb of Ouchy, is the remarkable **Olympic Museum** (open May–Sept: daily 10am–7pm; Oct–April: 10am–5pm), with its detailed documentation of everything connected with the Olympics.

MORGES

The attractive rural town of **Morges** (pop. 12,500) was founded in 1286 by Louis I of Savoy and turned into a military harbour by Bern at the end of the 17th century. Its centre, still largely intact, extends from the parish church, built in 1771, to the 13th-century castle, which now houses the Vaud Military Museum. On Saturday morning there is a lively food market set up among the cafés and shops in the pedestrian zone.

NYON

The next major town on this route, ★ **Nyon** (pop. 14,000), is best reached via a detour, the so-called **Route de Vignoble**, a delightful wine route that passes through a number of picturesque villages. Nyon is a pretty little town, which developed from the old Roman settlement of Noviodunum. The fascinating **Musée Romain** (open April–Oct: Tues–Sat 10am–noon, 2–5pm, Sun 10am–5pm; Nov–Mar: Tues–Sat 2–5pm, Sun 10am–5pm), well located in the excavated ruins of an ancient basilica, documents the days when Nyon was a Roman garrison.

Below: a Nyon vine
Bottom: the Musée Romain

A kilometre or two east of Nyon, set in lovely formal gardens, is the ★ **Château de Prangins**, built in the 1730s in the French style, and recently renovated and converted into a branch of the **Swiss National Museum** (open Tues–Sun 10am–5pm), devoted to the history of Switzerland in the 18th and 19th centuries. The collection is an interesting one, and there are often entertaining special events to highlight the historical facts.

Just before you reach Geneva, the castle in ★ **Coppet** (pop. 1,600) had a famous owner at the beginning of the 19th century – Madame de Staël (1766–1817), who turned it into a favourite meeting place for Europe's poets and philosophers. The castle is now a museum.

11: The Holiday Corner of Switzerland

Basel – Zürich – Chur – Julierpass – St Moritz (284km/176 miles)

Map on pages 44–5

This long, diagonal route leads from Basel in the northwest right across Switzerland to its southeastern corner and the most attractive part of Grisons – the famous Engadine. This route is full of contrasts, with the mountains gradually approaching all the time. At the Zürichsee (Lake Zürich) the land is still quite flat, but by the time the route reaches the Walensee, the jagged peaks of the Churfirsten are visible high above the lake. Chur, the old town on the Upper Rhine, marks the beginning of a curvaceous route across the mountain passes of Grisons. There are rewarding detours all the way; to Einsiedeln, for instance, Glarus, or Davos. With so much to see and visit, plan for at least two overnight stays on this trip, if not more.

Artist's inspiration
Drawn not only by the beauty of nature but also by its power, J.M.W. Turner was inspired by his visits to Switzerland. The Zürichsee was the inspiration for some of his best 'skyscapes'.

Brugg stained glass

ANCIENT TREASURES

Around 10km (6 miles) outside Basel *(see page 20)*, not far from Augst, is the most important Roman excavation site in Switzerland: ★ **Augusta Raurica**, with an impressive theatre and ruined temples. The **site museum** (open April–Sept: Tues–Sun 10am–noon, 1.30–6pm; Oct–Mar until 5pm), housed inside the reconstructed Römerhaus, holds lots of treasures.

Beyond the Bözberg (569m/1,867ft), at an ancient crossing-point over the River Aare, lies **Brugg** (pop. 9,000), a town with an attractive historic centre. More important from the cultural point of view are two monuments nearby: one is the church of the former abbey of **Königsfelden**, a masterpiece of Swiss Mendicant Order architecture with some interesting ★ **stained-glass windows** in the choir; the other is the Roman amphitheatre of **Vindonissa**, which once accommodated nearly 10,000 spectators. The Vindonissa Museum in Brugg contains finds from the Roman encampment here.

BADEN

There are more Roman traces in **Baden** (pop. 15,000), where the sulphur springs were renowned for their curative properties during antiquity and the thermal baths are still popular today. There's a good view of the old part of town from the Hochbrücke, which connects Baden with neighbouring Wettingen. The **Museum Langmatt** (open April–Oct: Tues–Sat 2–6pm, Sun 10am–noon, 2–6pm) is an absolute must for art lovers. The villa belonging to Sidney and Jenny Brown now houses a magnificent ★ **painting collection**, including several works by French Impressionists.

Below: Baden housing
Bottom: Turner's Zürich

LAKE ZÜRICH AND RAPPERSWIL

This region close to the Alps contains numerous beautiful lakes. The part of the route beyond Zürich *(see page 39)* runs along the northern shore of the ★ **Zürichsee** (89sq km/34sq miles), a product of Ice Age glaciation. Things are a lot warmer these days: the climate is so mild that wine grapes can be grown on the lake's northern shore. There are lots of expensive lakeside villas in this south-facing section, which local people refer to as Zürich's 'gold coast'.

★ **Rapperswil** (pop. 7,500) is pleasantly situated on a small peninsula. The town is dominated by its imposing 12th-century castle and the much-

Map on pages 44–5

With the help of ravens
When the hermit Meinrad withdrew to the forest he was kept alive by food brought to him by two ravens. When he was murdered by bandits, it was the ravens who tracked them down and screamed so mercilessly that they confessed.

The Klöntalersee

altered and restored 13th-century parish church. From the castle parapet there's an excellent view over the lake and to the **Etzel** (1,098m/3,600ft).

BENEDICTINE HERITAGE

It was in 1358 that Rudolf of Habsburg had the first wooden bridge built at Rapperswil for pilgrims headed for **Einsiedeln** (pop. 10,000), the most famous pilgrimage centre in Switzerland. Situated 20km (12 miles) from Rapperswil, it lies amid peaceful Alpine scenery not far from the Sihlsee reservoir.

The Benedictine monastery dates back to the 10th century. The first monastery was built in 934 above the remains of the hermitage of St Meinrad, who was murdered in 861. It was during the 17th and 18th centuries that the complex was given its present-day appearance.

The huge, double-towered ★★ **monastery church** (1719–35) is considered the finest baroque structure in the country. The stucco work and ceiling frescoes were done by the Asam brothers from Munich, and the magnificent wrought-iron choir screen came from the workshop of Vinzenz Nussbaumer. The neoclassical Lady Chapel (1817) contains a late 15th-century image of the Virgin and Child.

DETOUR TO GLARUS

Further along the route, the town of ★ **Näfels** (pop. 4,000) lies at the entrance to ★ **Glarus**, a region entirely surrounded by mountains. It was here in 1388 that the men of Glarus gained their independence by defeating a Habsburg army.

This tiny mountain canton has a lot to offer in the way of sights, one such being the impressive **Klöntalersee** at the foot of the Glärnisch (2,914m/9,560ft). Nearby, the car-free holiday resort of **Braunwald** is superbly situated above the Linth valley; the Serftal, with the small village of **Elm**, is also worth a visit.

The capital of the canton, also called **Glarus** (pop. 6,000), had to be partially rebuilt after a

serious fire in 1861, caused by the notorious *Föhn*
wind *(see page 11)*.

A trip from here to the ★ **Klausen Pass**
(1,948m/6,391ft) and into the neighbouring Reuss
valley (round trip from Näfels 70km/50 miles)
provides magnificent views of the high, glacier-
covered peaks of the Glarus Alps (Tödi, 3,614m/
11,857ft; Clariden, 3,268m/10,722ft).

SULPHUR SPRINGS

The town of ★ **Sargans**, at the junction of the main
northern and western routes in Grisons, is dominated by an imposing 12th-century ★ **castle**. Further on, **Bad Ragaz** (pop. 4,600) is one of the
most traditional health spas in Switzerland. The
water here was praised by no less a person than
the great Paracelsus (1493–1541).

The original spring at **Bad Pfäfers** is idyllically
situated amid some wild scenery 4km (2 miles)
further up the valley. The monks from the Benedictine monastery of the same name built a thermal bath for themselves here during the 15th
century; in those days the patients were lowered
into the waters on ropes.

Nearby, ★ **Tamina Gorge**, along which patients
had to walk to reach the waters, is quite breathtaking. A paved route leads to the sulphur springs
(open May–Oct: daily 10am–6pm).

*Below: Bad Ragaz church
Bottom: spectacular Sargans*

Map
on pages
44–5

The Magic Mountain
It was during a trip to Davos in 1912 that the German author Thomas Mann conceived his famous novel *The Magic Mountain*.

Snowboarding near Klosters

VISITING THE PRÄTTIGAU

The attractive Prättigau begins to the east of **Landquart**. At the foot of the Rätikon massif is the holiday resort of ★ **Klosters**, rather unassuming in relation to its famous neighbour **Davos** (pop. 13,000), 43km (27 miles) away on the other side of the watershed. The region is very popular with hikers in summer, but it's in wintertime that everything gets really crowded here: there are 320km (198 miles) of ski piste alone.

The Weissfluh (2,840m/9,317ft) has a cable car link and provides the most commanding view of the area. Some popular excursions, featuring superb scenery, include the ★ **Sertigtal** and the Dischmatal.

PEAKS AND VIEWS

The journey into what is perhaps Switzerland's most attractive region, the Engadine, begins with the steep ascent from **Chur** *(see page 59)* to the Acl'Alva watershed (1,546m/5,072ft). There's a large holiday and sports region up here, consisting of **Parpan**, **Valbella**, the idyllic **Il Lai** and **Lai**. With the magnificent peaks of the Oberhalbstein in the distance, the route then continues down to **Tiefencastel** (pop. 300). This village has a surprise in store: 2km (1 mile) outside on a small rise lies the ★ **Church of Mistail**. This ancient building, with three semi-circular apses, dates from the 8th century and is the best-preserved Carolingian church in the country.

Tiefencastel is a major junction, connecting with the newly-resurfaced Schinstrasse (13km/8 miles to Thusis) and also with the ★★ **Albula Pass** (2,312m/7,585ft) which leads to St Moritz. This route is far less frequently used than the Julier Pass *(see next page)*, and the landscape is a lot more attractive. Two particularly striking villages along the way are Filisur and ★ **Bravuogn**.

This route is closed to motor traffic in winter when another form of transport takes over – the sledge. The railway connection with the Engadine also passes through the Albula Valley, and the rail tunnel beneath the watershed of the Inn is 6km (4 miles) long. The Bergün–Preda section of the line in particular, with its lofty viaducts and winding tunnels, represents one of the most daring feats of railway engineering to be found anywhere in the Alps.

Star Attractions
• Albula Pass
• Upper Engadine

THE UPPER ENGADINE

The trip through the Oberhalbstein (Surses) up to the Julier Pass is accompanied by a fine view of the high Alps. The village of **Savognin** (pop. 850) on the way is a popular holiday resort with a well-developed winter sports industry. Up on the ★ **Julier Pass** (2,284m/7,493ft) itself, the remains of two pillars, on the left and right of the road, stand as reminders that this route was also taken by the Romans.

Below: Tiefencastle
Bottom: Silvaplana

The trip down into the valley on the other side features a fantastic view, above **Silvaplana** (pop. 800), of the ★★ **Upper Engadine**, with its deep blue lakes, forested mountain slopes and green meadows dwarfed by the massive, icy peaks above. The small village of **Sils Maria** was where the German philosopher Friedrich Nietzsche (1844–1900) wrote *Also Sprach Zarathustra*. His home, near the Edelweiss Hotel, contains souvenirs of his life.

The route eventually arrives in the internationally-known resort of **St Moritz** (see page 87).

Map on pages 44–5

12: The Upper and Lower Engadine

Landeck – Scuol – St Moritz – Maloja Pass – Chiavenna (155km/96 miles)

The last bear

Many bears still roamed the Engadine in the late 19th century, but the last one – the last in all of Switzerland – was shot by two hunters from Scuol in 1904 in the Val Mingèr, which is now part of the Swiss National Park.

The Engadine is 4,000m (13,120ft) high and 50km (31 miles) long, and combines sunshine and stunning views with the delights of cosmopolitan resorts like St Moritz. The part of it known as the Upper Engadine is the home of Switzerland's *Romansh*-speaking community. It is a self-enclosed Alpine landscape with a dry climate and what many consider to be the best and most varied scenery in Switzerland – enhanced in particular by the numerous lakes extending from St Moritz to the Maloja Pass. The Lower Engadine is quite different. It is a deep valley between high, jagged mountains (their peaks are reminiscent of those in the Dolomites), with the same excellent climate as the Upper Engadine but with considerably less tourism.

This route down the River Inn can be done easily by bicycle if you feel like some exercise. The roads here aren't built for fast, through traffic, and nor is the landscape: there are far too many bends and far too much to see on either side. Anyone planning to include the valleys to the south – Val Müstair, Puschlav and Bergell – will certainly need to plan for at least one overnight stay.

The Lower Engadine valley

THE LOWER ENGADINE

Travelling into the Engadine from Austria, the Swiss border is reached beneath the Hochfinstermünz, 33km (20 miles) from Landeck. A little further on, the road branches off to the right, towards **Samnaun**. This winter sports resort, consisting of several small hamlets, is also an attractive destination in the summer months: it sells duty-free spirits, tobacco and perfume.

The first proper municipality in the Lower Engadine is ★ **Scuol** (pop. 1,800), which together with Tarasp and Vulpera makes up a popular holiday and health resort. High on a rocky outcrop above the Inn, ★ **Schloss Tarasp** can be seen for miles around; it dates from the 11th century and contains an interesting furniture collection.

Those eager to ascend a mountain at this point have a wide range of choices. The easiest way to get a great view is to take the cable car up to **Motta Naluns** (2,146m/7,040ft), but if you're planning to hike, go to the unusually-named hamlet of **S-carl**, 12km (7 miles) from Scuol; it's the ideal starting-point for hikes into the Swiss National Park *(see below)*. Other popular excursions in this region include the mountain villages of **Ftan** and **Sent**.

The village of ★ **Guarda**, set on a sunny slope high above the valley road, is known as 'the jewel of the Engadine'. Its attractive houses, cobbled streets and pretty fountains form an atmospheric ensemble – all of it framed against the backdrop of the jagged mountains of the Lower Engadine.

SWISS NATIONAL PARK

The village of **Vernez** (pop. 900) grew up at the foot of an old pass route across the Fuorn to Val Müstair. Since 1909 this route has crossed the ★ **Swiss National Park** (open June–Oct: Sun–Fri 9am–noon, 1.30–6.30pm, Sat until 5pm), situated southeast of the Inn, between the Val Trupchun and the Val S-carl. Here, nature has been left entirely to itself, and visitors have to keep to the marked routes. There are 650 different species of plants, and over 30 kinds of mammals and birds,

Below: Guarda façade with Romansh inscription
Bottom: the Swiss National Park

Map on pages 44–5

A March festival
On 1 March, the children's festival of *Chalandamarz* (or *Calanda mars*) takes place in many villages. This begins the Romany New Year celebrations and takes the form of a colourful spring parade in the old Romansh tradition.

Zernez church spire

including the bearded vulture, which faced extinction before it was brought here and encouraged to breed in 1991.

THE UPPER ENGADINE

The ★**Pass del Fuorn** (2,149m/7,050ft) lies above the watershed leading to Val Müstair, an extensive hiking region. The town of **Müstair** (pop. 800) itself is just next to the Italian border, 39km (24 miles) from Zernez; its ★★★**Benedictine convent** is very famous. The church, which originally had a flat roof, was renovated in Gothic style during the 15th century. A number of well-preserved frescoes dating from Carolingian times (c. 800) have been uncovered on its walls.

A short way beyond Zernez, near S-chanf, the route crosses from the Lower to the ★★**Upper Engadine**. The mountain slopes recede, and the narrow valley widens out into a flat plateau. The settlements here generally face south. ★**Zuoz** (pop. 1,200), the best-preserved of the villages in the upper reaches of the Inn, is a good example. Its Dorfplatz and fountain are atmospheric, and the late Gothic church with a pointed spire contains fine stained glass by Augusto Giacometti.

The old capital of the Upper Engadine is **Samedan** (pop. 2,500). This attractive town has a striking 17th-century church. The Haus Planta, a residence of an ancient family, with the bear's paw crest, houses an interesting cultural centre (Fundaziun Planta) with a *Romansh* library.

PONTRESINA

The Val Bernina opens up to the south. A few miles in lies ★**Pontresina** (pop. 1,600), a traditional holiday resort. The pretty Engadine houses are complemented by several dignified-looking hotels dating from the early days of tourism, and the Alpine backdrop is provided by the high peaks in the Val Roseg. Two rivals for the best view of the Engadine mountains are ★**Muottas Muragl** (2,453m/8,048ft) and ★**Diavolezza** (2,973m/9,754ft), both easily reached by cable car.

THE BERNINA PASS

There are also breathtaking views across mountains and valleys from the dramatic ★★ **Bernina Pass** (2,328m/7,638ft), 24km (14 miles) from Samedan. This pass connects the Engadine with the ★ **Puschlav**, or Val Poschiavo, one of the three Italian-speaking valleys in Grisons. The trip across the pass is quite an experience in itself, but the descent on the other side is even more memorable. The route comes down from eternal ice and passes vineyards and chestnut groves (a difference in altitude of around 2,000m/6,500ft).

If you're not in any hurry, take a trip on the **Rhätische Bahn** railway; it gives you time to soak up all the scenery. The section just before Alp Grüm (2,091m/6,860ft) and down to Poschiavo (pop. 3,300) is delightful.

ST MORITZ

★ **St Moritz** (pop. 6,000) is the favourite haunt of the jet set, and it's more common to see millionaires in the streets than farmers. This town has hosted the Winter Olympics twice now, and each year, on three Sundays in February, the famous horse races are held on the frozen St Moritzersee. This world-famous cosmopolitan metropolis is also a health spa: there's a modern and very luxurious sanatorium in the suburb of Bad.

Star Attractions
• **Müstair convent**
• **Upper Engadine**
• **Bernina Pass**

Below: Zuoz stained glass
Bottom: a Bernina view

Map
on pages
44–5

Map on pages 44–5

The art of travel posters
Beautiful art nouveau and art deco travel posters were designed from the turn of the 20th century to the 1930s to entice visitors to Switzerland. Reproductions and postcards are still available and make wonderful souvenirs.

The so-called 'Dorf' section of St Moritz – the site of the old settlement above the lake – is far more of a town than a village these days. Its leaning tower, part of a church demolished in the 19th century, looks rather forlorn among all the high-rise hotels. The ★ **Engadine Museum** (open Mon–Fri 9.30am–noon, 2–5pm, Sun 10am–noon) effectively brings the past to life with its collection of magnificent interiors dating from the 16th to the 19th centuries.

The painter Giovanni Segantini (1859–99) spent the last years of his life here, and the cupola-shaped **Segantini Museum** (open Tues–Sat 9am–12.30pm, 2.30–5pm, Sun 10.30am–12.30pm, 2.30–4.30pm) is devoted to his life and work.

EVERY KIND OF SPORT

It is probably superfluous to mention that St Moritz caters for absolutely every kind of sport, both in summer and winter. One very popular event at the moment is the Engadine Ski Marathon, held in March; 10,000 people took part in it recently. The most famous peak for skiing is the **Piz Nair** (3,057m/10,030ft). Those eager to go very high up should take the cable car to the **Piz Corvatsch** (3,303m/10,837ft); its valley station can be reached from Silvaplana (pop. 800

The view from Piz Nair

along a short access road. The panorama from the top, extending from the Bernse to the Ötztaler Alps, is utterly breathtaking.

HIKING ROUTE

The best way to experience the full beauty of the Engadine, however, is on foot. One very good hiking route is the Via Engiadina, which runs along the left-hand side of the valley from St Moritz to Maloja (about 6 hours). Another route is from Sils Maria *(see page 83)* to the ★ **Fextal**, which is now a nature reserve. A rewarding objective for experienced mountain climbers is the **Piz de la Margna** (3,159m/10,364ft), a famous landmark of the Engadine (a climb of about 4–5 hours).

THE BERGELL

On the threshold of the ★ **Maloja Pass**, the Upper Engadine lake region turns into the ★★ **Bergell**, or Val Bregaglia. The change of scenery here is swift and stunning: on one side there's a broad basin gouged by glaciers, and on the other a deep and narrow valley. The hotels and chalets of the Engadine are replaced in Italian-speaking Bergell by old, huddled villages such as Vicosoprano, Stampa and Bondo. The houses with their *sgraffito* decoration are typical of this region.

Alongside local history, the **Talmuseum** in **Stampa** also documents the work of the Giacomettis, a local family of artists whose most famous member was the sculptor and painter, Alberto (1901–66). On the way out of the village there's the surprising Palazzo Castelmur, an Italian-Moorish-style building constructed in the mid-19th century, complete with battlements.

Finally, one brief but unmissable detour is from Spino through a magnificent chestnut grove and up to ★ **Soglio**. This village is not only famous for its well-preserved old houses but also for its view of the jagged, granite peaks across the valley, and of the Piz Badile (3,308m/10,853ft).

It's not far now to **Chiavenna** (over the border in Italy), where this route ends.

Early 20th-century travel posters

ST. MORITZ

STRANDBAD
INTERLAKEN

Map on pages 44–5

13: The Eiger, Mönch and Jungfrau

Bern – Thun – Interlaken – Susten Pass – Wassen (136km/84 miles)

The Alpine trio
Eiger, Mönch and Jungfrau (ogre, monk and virgin) are the three giant Alps always thought of together, and seen – on a clear day – from miles around.

You can see them from Bern on a clear day: the distant, icy peaks of the Bernse Alps. They form a grand backdrop to the Bernr Oberland, that typically Swiss picture-book landscape at the upper reaches of the Aare. Grindelwald, Wengen, Adelboden and Interlaken are all names that conjure up winter holidays. Everyone has probably heard of the notorious north face of the Eiger, too; and Europe's highest railway station is on the Jungfraujoch. The food in this area is delicious as well: golden-brown *Rösti* or a *Bernr Platte* are just two of the mouth-watering local specialities. It's hard to digest so many visual – and culinary – impressions in just one day, so allow time for at least one overnight stay.

Thun castle

THUN

There are quite a lot of cows along this route, so to get yourself in the mood, consider visiting the **National Milk Museum** (open April–Oct: daily 2–5pm), situated only 19km (11 miles) outside Bern *(see page 25)* in the village of **Kiesen**. It features a reconstruction of an 18th-century cheesemaker's premises.

The town of ★ **Thun** (pop. 40,000), on the lake of the same name, is the gateway to the Bernr Oberland. The old section of the town is dominated by the ★ **castle**, a Zähringer structure dating from 1191. Its keep houses a **Historical Museum** (April, May, Oct: daily 10am–5pm; June–Sep: 9am–6pm), with collections ranging from prehistoric finds to suits of armour.

To the south of Thun, beside the lake, is Schloss Schadau (1854), with its **Gastronomy Museum** (open Tues and Thurs 2–5pm) and restaurant.

For the onward journey to Interlaken, there's a choice of two routes around Lake Thun. The route along the northern shore provides better views of the Bernse Alps and also goes past the

Beatus Caves (open April–Oct: daily 9.30am–5.30pm). A 1-km (⅔-mile) long tunnel leads to this cave system, which was inhabited in prehistoric times. Waterfalls and some fantastic stalactites and stalagmites make any visit here a memorable experience.

Star Attraction
•Jungfrau

THE SIMMENTAL AND GSTAAD

The idyllic ★ **Simmental**, with its lush, green meadows and picturesque villages, opens out to the west near Spiez, and is an ideal region for hiking. **Gstaad** (pop. 1,800) lies 50km (30 miles) away from Spiez in the Saanenland, beyond the Saanenmöser watershed (1,279m/4,196ft). Gstaad is a famous holiday resort and a popular meeting place for members of the aristocracy and high society. In winter the beautiful people rub shoulders with ordinary folk on the lifts and pistes; during *après-ski* round here it's always reassuring to have a full wallet.

INTERLAKEN AND THE JUNGFRAU

Not far away is one of the very first tourist resorts in Switzerland: ★ **Interlaken** (pop. 5,000), so named because it lies between Lake Thun and Lake Brienz. The view from the tree-lined hiking route on the ★★ **Jungfrau** (4,158m/13,641ft) is

Below: chic Gstaad
Bottom: the Beatus Caves

Map on pages 44–5

Below: Interlaken weir
Bottom: the Eiger, Mönch and Jungfrau

justly famous. The **Touristik-Museum** (open May–Oct: Tues–Sun 2–5pm) in Unterseen has a series of interesting and curious exhibits documenting the early days of tourism.

A major reason for the sudden increase in tourism was the improved access provided by the construction of numerous railways and cable-car routes. Today, some of these have become an attraction in their own right. Why not leave your car behind and explore the surrounding valleys by rail for a change?

GRINDELWALD AND MÜRREN

The town of ★★ **Grindelwald** (pop. 3,900) lies 20km (12 miles) from Interlaken, and the best view of it, framed against the backdrop of the ★★★ **Eiger** (3,970m/13,025ft), the Mettenberg and the Wetterhorn is from the cable-car station at the summit of the First (2,167m/7,110ft).

High up on sunny terraces above the valley of the White Lütschine are the villages of ★ **Wengen** and ★★ **Mürren**. They are doubly attractive as places to stay, because cars aren't allowed – visitors have to leave their vehicles in the valley below, and are thus forced to undergo a holiday free of stress and exhaust fumes.

An integral part of any stay here is a cable-car ride up to the ★★ **Schilthorn** (2,970m/9,744ft),

gives you one of the most magnificent views in a country where breathtaking views are almost-commonplace.

The ★★ **Jungfraubahn** is the ultimate mountain railway. Opened in 1912, 9.3km (5 miles) long and mostly consisting of tunnels, it overcomes gradients of up to 25 percent to reach the Jungfraujoch station (3,454m/ 11,332ft), covering a difference in altitude of 1,400m (4,593ft) in the process. From the ridge between the Mönch (4,099m/13,448ft) and the Jungfrau (4,158m/ 13,642ft) there's a fascinating view across high mountain peaks and the great Alpine glaciers, particularly the ★ **Aletsch Glacier** *(see page 98).*

RAILWAYS AND WATERFALLS

The town of ★ **Brienz** (pop. 2,900) on the northern shore of the Brienzersee, is a popular holiday resort and also a woodcarving centre. Rail enthusiasts will enjoy riding up to the ★ **Brienzer Rothorn** (2,350m/7,710ft) on Switzerland's only surviving steam-operated mountain railway – and if the weather happens to be fine, it can be a really exhilarating experience.

On the opposite bank of the Brienzersee, the ★ **Giessbachfälle** (falls) make an equally popular excursion. The water thunders dramatically down a 300-m (984-ft) drop via 14 different levels and into the lake. This is a worthwhile detour, especially when combined with a boat trip.

SWISS OPEN-AIR MUSEUM

Just 4km (2 miles) outside Brienz, near Hofstetten, is the ★ **Swiss Open-Air Museum** (open April–Oct: daily 10am–5pm) at Ballenberg, where there is an interesting display of rural architecture. The farmhouses and other buildings have been brought here from all over Switzerland, complete with traditional interiors, and there are daily demonstrations of traditional crafts in every building. It is especially interesting to note how little living space there was in the huge structures that also had to serve as grain stores and house the

Star Attractions
•**Grindelwald**
•**The Eiger**
•**Mürren**
•**the Schilthorn**
•**the Jungfraubahn**

Mystery Park
In this new theme park, Erich von Däniken has brought the great mysteries of the world together. Visitors pay virtual visits to the sites of the world's mysteries, travelling back through time to the roots of their different cultures, and making new discoveries or deciding on their own explanations.

Giessbachfälle

Map
on pages
44–5

A temporary death at the falls
Arthur Conan Doyle often stayed in Meiringen and in 1891 set the demise of his famous detective, Sherlock Holmes, in the chasm of the Reichenbach Falls. Under pressure from his fans, however, he resurrected him more than a decade later. A small museum in the sleuth's memory can be visited at the English church of Meiringen.

hay, food supplies, equipment, tools and animals. In one building, you can still smell the smokehouse that was in the middle.

Meiringen (pop. 2,800), the main town in the Haslital, is an ideal base for hiking or skiing trips. It is directly connected to the *piste* region up on the Hasliberg. The principal sight here is a little further down the valley: the 1.5-km (1-mile) long ★ **Aare Gorge**, a grandiose natural monument. Nearby, at the end of the Rosenlaui Valley, are the **Reichenbach Falls**, which can be visited by cable ropeway. The falls were made famous by Sir Arthur Conan Doyle's fictional creation Sherlock Holmes *(see box)*.

IMPRESSIVE ALPENSTRASSEN

The small town of **Innertkirchen** (pop. 1,000) lies at the foot of the pass over the ★★ **Grimsel** (2,165m/7,103ft) and the ★★ **Susten** (2,224m/7,296ft), which lead into the upper valley of the Rhône and the Reuss valley respectively. Both routes are considered to be among the finest *Alpenstrassen* in Switzerland, and pass a lot of impressive high-mountain scenery.

From the tunnel at the top of the ★★ **Susten Pass** (2,224m/7,296ft), the route continues down through the Meiental to Wassen, where it connects with Route 6 *(see page 51)*.

Crags above the Susten Pass

14: The Vineyards and Glaciers of the Valais

Martigny – Sion – Brig – Furka Pass – Andermatt (159km/98 miles)

The southern canton of Valais is full of contrasts. It contains the country's three highest mountains – the Dufourspitze (4,634m/15,203ft), Monte Rosa (4,634m/15,203ft) and the Matterhorn (4,478m/14,692ft). It has the biggest glaciers too, but tomatoes, apricots and grapes grow quite happily in the Rhône valley below. A massive concrete dam, the largest in the world, has been constructed in the Val d'Hérémence, and the future of tourism is being tested out – architecturally at least – in Crans-Montana. The nearby Lötsch Valley is famous for cherishing its ancient traditions. The trip to the Furka Pass can be done in a day, but anyone eager to visit any of the valleys on the way should organise at least one night's accommodation.

FORTIFIED HILLS

Two fortified hills on the right bank of the Rhône are the distinguishing feature of **Sion/Sitten** (pop. 25,000), 28km (17 miles) beyond Martigny *(see page 69)*. By far the most striking building in the old section of the town beneath the castle rock is the 15th-century cathedral of **Notre-Dame-du-Glarier**, with its mighty Romanesque tower. The Rathaus (1657–65), with an astronomical tower clock, is also worthy of note. The fortress-like complex of the Majorie (1536) contains the Valais Art Museum and the **Archaeological Museum** (open Tues–Sun 10am–noon, 2–5pm).

In contrast to Schloss Tourbillon, built in 1294 and in ruins today, the ★ **Valeria** still looks fortified and medieval. The walled complex is dominated by the Romanesque-Gothic collegiate church; the 14th-century organ is thought to be the oldest playable one in the world. Several rooms house the ★ **Valeria Museum** (undergoing alteration; open Tues–Sun 10am–noon), a rich collection based on medieval cultural history.

Star Attractions
• Grimsel
• Susten
• Susten Pass

Below: the Valeria seen from Schloss Tourbillon
Bottom: the Valeria organ

Map
on pages
44–5

Sunny Valais
Valais is the sunniest and
driest canton in Switzer-
land, and thus produces some of the
country's best wines.

The Pyramides d'Euseigne

EXCURSIONS FROM SION

There are several great places to visit in the surrounding area, such as the vineyards and pretty
houses around Saviès. The highlights of this
region, however, are the ★ **Val d'Hérens** and the
★ **Val d'Hérémence** with their typical Valais
mountain villages (Evolène, Les Haudères, La
Forclaz); the dark-brown, wooden houses contrast attractively with the snowy mountain peaks
in the background. The impressive 284-m (932-
ft) high concrete dam on the **Lac des Dix** at the
heart of the Val d'Hérémence was built in 1961,
and is the tallest gravity dam in the world.

Not far away there's a relic from the Ice Age:
the so-called **Pyramides d'Euseigne**, earth pillars protected from erosion by the flat stones
which cap them. Near St-Léonard there's another
natural wonder: a **subterranean lake**, signposted
as you leave the village. The lake, on which boat
trips can be taken, is 300m (984ft) long and up
to 22m (72ft) deep in places.

VINEYARDS AND PANORAMIC VIEWS

Just 10km (6 miles) further on, **Sierre** (pop.
15,000) lies some distance away from the Rhône
in the midst of extensive vineyards. This region
was inhabited during prehistoric times. Remains
of a Roman *castrum* have also been discovered
here. The 15th-century castle, a massive structure
with four corner-towers, stands as a reminder of
the time when the region was controlled by the
bishops of Sion; it was the residence of their
bailiffs. The 17th-century Maison de Courten contains a room commemorating the German poet
Rainer Maria Rilke (1875–1926), who stayed here
briefly in 1922. He spent the final few years of his
life in the nearby castle of Muzot.

Around 15km (9 miles) from Sierre, the sunny
holiday resort of **Crans-Montana** has everything
a visitor could wish for, including a panoramic
view of the entire Valais Alps; there are several
concrete, high-rise hotels here as well, however.

The 20-km (12-mile) long ★ **Val d'Anniviers**,
much admired for its scenic beauty, connects with

the opposite side of the Rhône valley. Beyond Sierre, the Pfynwald, which unfortunately is now suffering from *Waldsterben* (trees dying because of pollution), forms the linguistic border between the Upper and Lower Valais. Above the entrance to the Dalatal is ★**Leuk** (pop. 3,000), an attractive and well-preserved old town. Below it on a small terrace is the fine baroque ★**Ringacker Chapel** (1694).

The ★★**Lötsch Valley**, one of the most delightful and least discovered parts of the Valais, is also a rewarding place to visit.

A VISIT TO THE MATTERHORN

A detour out of the Rhône valley near **Visp** (pop. 6,400) is almost inevitable, because one of the most famous and most-photographed mountains in the world lies just a short distance away: the ★★★ **Matterhorn** (4,478m/14,692ft). It was first climbed in 1865, under tragic circumstances, by Edward Whymper and his team. Four of his party fell to their deaths on the descent. Since that time, however, the Matterhorn has been every ambitious mountain-climber's dream.

Motorists can only drive as far as Täsch, 30km (18 miles) away from Visp; transport from there to ★★**Zermatt** (pop. 5,000) is taken care of by a railway. Shortly before arriving at Zermatt –

Star Attractions
• Lötsch Valley
• the Matterhorn
• Zermatt

Below: the Val d'Anniers
Bottom: bathers at Leukerbad

Map
on pages
44–5

*Below: mountaineers'
graves in Zermatt
Bottom: Saas-Fee*

assuming the weather is good – the mountain comes into view. The first good view of the splendid panorama, however, is from the rack railway to ★ **Gornergrat** (3,131m/10,272ft). Those keen on going higher can do so via cable car, to the Kleiner Matterhorn (3,820m/12,533ft) on the Plateau Rosa (a summer-skiing region).

SAAS-FEE AND BRIG

Zermatt is far better known than its unjustly-neglected neighbour ★★ **Saas-Fee** (pop. 1,300) at the heart of the Saasertal, 26km (16 miles) from Visp (car park at entrance to town). For a really magnificent Alpine panorama, take the 45-minute walk from Saas-Grund along the ★ **Kapellenweg** and up to the village beneath the Fee Glacier.

The town of **Brig** (pop. 4,000) had its appearance changed distinctively by one man, Kaspar Jodok Stockalper (1609–91), the uncrowned 'king of the Simplon'. An extremely rich merchant, he used much of his wealth, between 1658 and 1678, to build the ★ **Stockalperschloss** (guided tours available), the most important baroque palace in Switzerland. Its three enormous onion-domed towers dominate the landscape.

Around 45km (28 miles) to the southwest of Brig is the highest peak in the whole of Switzerland, the **Dufourspitze** (4,634m/15,203ft). Its summit was first reached by an Englishman in 1855.

THE SIMPLON PASS

The history of Brig is also closely connected with that of the ★ **Simplon Pass** (2,005m/6,578ft), which became important early on as a way of crossing into Lombardy. Napoleon had the pass route turned into a road, and at the beginning of the 20th century the 19-km (12-mile) long rail tunnel was mined out of the rock. Today, the Simplon route is well used and kept in excellent condition. The old hospice here was founded in 1235, and extended in the 17th century.

The 28-km (17-mile) long ★ **Aletsch Glacier** is one of the natural wonders of the Alps. It has an overall surface area of 86sq km/33sq miles. Commanding views of this mighty river of ice can be had from the Belalp (2,094m/6,870ft, ropeway from Blatten, 9km/5 miles from Brig).

Good bases for hiking trips in this region are ★ **Riederalp** (1,943m/6,375ft) and Bettmeralp (1,950m/6,398ft), reached by cable car from the Rhône valley. Another cable-car link leads from Fiesch to the mountain with the best view in the area, the ★ **Eggishorn** (2,926m /9,600ft). Opposite, on the way back into the valley, is the particularly attractive Valais village of ★ **Ernen**, with numerous buildings dating from the 15th to 17th centuries as well as a fine Gothic church (1518).

THE GOMS AND THE RHÔNE GLACIER

The section of the Upper Valais here is known as the ★ **Goms**. All the villages are on the northern side of the river. Some, especially Niederwald, Reckingen and Münster, have fine old houses and baroque churches.

In Gletsch the mighty ★ **Rhône Glacier** comes into view. Far below in the valley, the serpentine shape of the Furkastrasse can be seen, leading straight up to the glacier. The ★ **Furka Pass** (2,431m/7,976ft) marks the transition from the Goms to the Urserental, which the route now follows as far as **Andermatt** *(see page 51)*.

Star Attraction
• Saas-Fee

Local traditions
Traditions are very important in the Lötsch Valley, especially on 'Dirty Thursday' when the *Roitschäggättä* ('smoke-blackened ones') make their way noisily through the streets wearing frightening wooden masks. This procession, held on the Sunday after Corpus Christi (mid-June), also includes a detachment of soldiers in Napoleonic uniform, known as the *Herrgottsgrenadiere*.

Looking out from the Furka Pass

Architecture and the Arts

During any trip to Switzerland one thing quickly becomes clear: the greatest monuments here have been created by nature rather than by humans. Pompous avenues, triumphal arches and other edifices left by emperors and kings in an attempt to gain some kind of immortality are conspicuous by their absence. In their place there is interesting cultural variety, which is reflected in the cuisine as well as the architecture. The Swiss are influenced by foreign ideas but never abandon their own.

ARCHITECTURE AND SCULPTURE

Swiss architecture began in the Stone Age, and the best place to gain an impression of what the earliest prehistoric lake-dwellings looked like is the Landesmuseum in Zürich. The Celtic Helvetian golden treasure discovered near Erstfeld in the Reuss Valley is also impressive. Ruined buildings remain at most of the old Roman towns and camps – Aventicum (Avenches), Noviodumum (Nyon), Octodurus (Martigny), Vindonissa (near Brugg) and Augusta Raurica (near Basel).

Influences from abroad are particularly evident in medieval architecture, the period when the Confederation was taking shape. The oldest religious buildings in Switzerland are the 6th-century baptistery in Riva San Vitale in Ticino, and the monastery church of St John in Müstair, with rare Carolingian frescoes (c. 800). The most important legacy of the early Middle Ages is the profusion of monasteries and abbeys, such as at St-Maurice (c. 515) and St Gallen (c. 700).

Romanesque: The Romanesque period (c. 900–1200) saw the construction of a great number of religious buildings in Switzerland, such as the Grossmünster in Zürich and the cathedral in Chur. The former collegiate church in Romainmôtier is very Burgundian. There are some fine examples of Romanesque sculpture in the cathedrals of Geneva (capitals) and Basel (Gallus Portal), and the Landesmuseum in Zürich has a comprehensive collection of wood carvings from

The Laténium

The Laténium Archaeological Park and Museum in Hautrive near Neuchâtel exhibits 50,000 years of prehistory and history in the original settings. Found underground and underwater, the exhibits cover the period from Neanderthal man to the Middle Ages. Named after La Tène, which, from Ireland to Romania, marks the Celtic civilisation of the Second Iron Age (www.latenium.ch).

Opposite: St Gallen library
Below: Schloss Oberhof

that period. However, the most important Romanesque masterpiece in Switzerland is the well-preserved wooden ceiling (1160) in the church of Zillis, Grisons *(see page 61)*.

Below: Stein am Rhein
Bottom: the Entombment,
Fribourg cathdral

Gothic: The Gothic style arrived in Switzerland from France during the second half of the 13th century. Stylistically, the proud cathedral in Lausanne is on a par with the Northern French structures upon which it was based; the cathedrals in Fribourg and Geneva are worth mentioning, too. In German Switzerland, influences from South Germany are unmistakable. In Bern, the late Gothic Münster was begun in 1421 by Matthaeus Ensinger from Ulm. Ticino was always influenced by Lombardy, though Italian-style buildings were also constructed north of the Alps (e.g. the Ritterscher Palast in Luzern).

During the late Gothic period, the art of stained glass reached perfection, as evidenced by Königsfelden or the cloisters of the monasteries at Wettingen and Muri. The huge rose window in Lausanne cathedral is the earliest stained-glass window in the country, and dates from around 1235. One speciality of the late Gothic period is exemplified by the numerous triptychs; the cathedral in Chur contains a fine example by Jakob Russ, and several more can be admired in the churches of Grisons.

Renaissance: The Renaissance style (14th–17th century) appeared as the population grew wealthier and more independent. Nobles and rich merchants built magnificent houses. Religious structures were replaced by secular ones, and the new self-confidence resulted in the construction of several fine *Rathäuser* (town halls) – the ones in Basel and Geneva are particularly good examples. Hardly any religious buildings in Switzerland date from the Renaissance period; exceptions include the Hofkirche in Luzern, the domed church of Santa Croce in Riva San Vitale and the façade of San Lorenzo in Lugano.

Baroque: During the baroque era (17th century), church architecture reached a high point with the construction of several magnificent monasteries including St Gallen, Rheinau, Disentis, Einsiedeln, Muri and St Urban. Several exponents of the Vorarlberg School were active in church building, especially in the eastern regions. The Beer and Moosbrugger families were among architectural dynasties who left their mark on religious structures across the country.

Ticino architects were also active at this time – not so much in Switzerland, however, as across Europe. Marco of Carona built the cathedral in Milan; Solari built walls and towers for the Kremlin; Domenico Fontana (1543–1607) built the Lateran Palace in Rome, and his nephew Carlo Maderna (1556–1629) constructed the façade of St Peter's; Baldassare Longhena (1598–1682) was the greatest baroque architect in Venice; and Domenico Trezzini was commissioned by Peter the Great to build St Petersburg from scratch.

The baroque period in Switzerland left a few interesting buildings. They include the Zunfthaus Zur Meise in Zürich, the Erlacher Hof in Bern, the Palais Besenval in Solothurn and the Maison de Saussure in Geneva. The only example of a consistently planned, late medieval town in Switzerland is the former market town of Carouge, just south of Geneva. It was commissioned in the late 17th century by Victor III of Savoy to break Geneva's trading monopoly.

> ### Farmhouses
> One very Swiss building is the farmhouse, and it has developed in very different ways in the different regions of the country. Emmental has the impressive Berner house, with its projecting hipped roof and balconies, often decorated with geraniums; the Engadine house can withstand the harshest winter because of its thick walls and tiny, low windows; the farmhouses in the Goms region (Upper Valais) and around the Gotthard follow a modular design, while the Aargauer thatched farmhouse has become something of a rarity. To get a full impression of all the different styles, visit the Swiss Open-Air Museum at Ballenberg (see page 93).

Renaissance stained glass, Romont

*Below: Bernadino Luini's
Portrait of a Lady
Bottom: Der Genfersee von
Chexbres by Hodler*

Neoclassical to Modern: After a neoclassical interlude in the mid-19th century, which produced such buildings as the Elisabethenkirche in Basel and the Grossmünsterkapelle and Federal Institute of Technology in Zürich, Swiss architecture during the late 19th and 20th centuries was largely confined to the construction of large residential and administrative complexes. A major creative force behind the International School of architecture, which dominated most building trends in the West, was Le Corbusier (Charles-Edouard Jeanneret, 1887–1965), who came from La Chaux-de-Fonds. He built very little in his native land, however; two exceptions are his glass house in Geneva, and the Le Corbusier centre in Zürich. Finally, Jean Tinguely, a 'kinetic' artist from Switzerland, has made a name for himself with his bizarre fountains and moving sculptures; two examples are the Heureka machine in Zürich, and the Fasnachtsbrunnen in Basel.

PAINTING

The most important paintings on Swiss soil are almost 1,200 years old, the Carolingian frescoes at Mustair. The painted wooden ceiling of Zillis (c. 1150), the oldest of its kind in Europe, is another supremely important cultural monument, as is the magnificent stained glass at Königsfelden

(1330). Konrad Witz (c. 1398–1445) is considered the father of Swiss landscape painting; and Bernardo Luini (c. 1480–1532) was one of Leonardo da Vinci's most gifted pupils. Later, Arnold Böcklin (1827–1908) became world-famous for such works as *The Isle of the Dead*, which prompted Rachmaninov to write a piece of music with the same title.

It was Ferdinand Hodler (1853–1918), however, whose powerful, unmistakable style – both in his portraits and the 'colour symphonies' of his landscapes – who gave Switzerland a voice in international art. He made his breakthrough in Paris, with his monumental work *Die Nacht (Night)*; to see this and other works, visit the Hodler exhibition in Zürich's Kunsthaus.

Perhaps the best known Swiss painter is Paul Klee (1879–1940), who grew up in Bern and satirised its rather stifling, petty bourgeois atmosphere in several of his early works. Later he developed his own highly pictorial language to express the spiritual essence of things, and has been acclaimed as one of the greatest artists of the 20th century. The biggest collection of his work can be seen in the Bern Kunstmuseum.

Jean Tinguely
Born in Fribourg in 1925, this popular sculptor pioneered kinetic art — metal constructions, sometimes powered by small motors, that move, clatter and ping, strike bottles or metal pans, make drawings and sometimes even destroy themselves.

Böcklin's Isle of the Dead

LITERATURE

Geneva was an important centre of Swiss-French literary life during the Enlightenment. The philosopher Jean-Jacques Rousseau (1712–78) was born there, and Voltaire lived in the city from 1755 to 1763. The brilliant Madame de Staël (1766–1817) made Schloss Coppet a centre of European intellectual life. Swiss-German literature began with the influential works of Paracelcus (1493–1541) and Huldrych Zwingli (1484–1531). The educationist Johann Heinrich Pestalozzi (1746–1827), and philosophers Gottfried Keller (1819–90) and Conrad Ferdinand Meyer (1825–98) also made important contributions. Carl Spitteler (1845–1924) wrote mythological epics in colloquial language, and is the only Swiss writer to have received the Nobel Prize. The Basel historian Jakob Burckhardt wrote several brilliant books during the late 19th century, including his world-famous *On the Civilisation of the Renaissance in Italy*. The writings of psychiatrist Carl Jung (1875–1961), who had chairs at both Basel and Zürich universities, have been highly influential.

Below: Friedrich Nietzsche Bottom: scenes such as this one of students taking maths lessons in a TB sanitorium inspired Thomas Mann's book The Magic Mountain

Several German writers produced much of their work in Switzerland. One was the philosopher, Friedrich Nietzsche, who had a professorship in Basel and spent much time in Sils Maria in the Engadine where the magnificent scenery inspired him to write *Also Sprach Zarathustra* in 1883, as a prelude to his 're-evaluation of all values'. The German writer Thomas Mann (1875–1955) set his influential work *Die Zauberberg (The Magic Mountain)* in a tuberculosis sanitorium in the resort of Davos.

A German writer much influenced by Nietzsche, Hermann Hesse (1877–1962), became a Swiss resident in 1923, living in Montagnola, Ticino. His work deals with the theme of human beings breaking out of accepted modes of thought and behaviour to find their essential spirit. His greatest novel, *The Glass Bead Game*, explores spiritual self-realisation and the duality between the contemplative and active life. Hesse lies buried in Collina d'Oro, southwest of Lugano.

Two Swiss dramatists made an important name for themselves during the 20th century: Max

Frisch (1911–91) who was also a major novelist, and Friedrich Dürrenmatt (1920–90). Frisch's central theme is the predicament of the complicated, sceptical individual in contemporary society, reflected particularly well in his novel *Homo Faber*, which has been made into a film. Dürrenmatt, who was much influenced by Berthold Brecht, exposes the absurdity and grotesqueness of human life in his plays, but without trying to interpret its significance. Frisch and Dürrenmatt are today considered the giants of contemporary Swiss-German literature.

MUSIC

Switzerland made little impact on the international music scene until the 20th century, when several composers appeared, including Arthur Honegger (1892–1955), Othmar Schoeck (1866–1957) and Frank Martin (1890–1974).

The country also has three world-famous orchestras: the Orchestra de la Suisse Romande, the Züricher Kammerorchester, and the Festival Strings Luzern. Some of the country's chamber ensembles have also made a name for themselves, such as the Camerata Bern. The Engadiner Kantorei is a well-known choir, and has made several internationally well-received recordings.

Festivals and Folklore

Despite industrialisation and the computer age, old traditions are still kept very much alive in Switzerland – and not only for the tourists. The *Fasnacht* (carnival) in Basel and the *Sechseläuten* ('six o'clock ringing') in Zürich are two of the best-known events, but the Swiss celebrate a vast range of other festivals throughout the year.

In the heart of the Alps, where German, French, Italian and *Romansh* cultures converge, varied customs can be found in the market places, at festivals or simply as part of ordinary domestic life. In Fribourg, La Gruyère or in the eastern area of Appenzell, for example, alpine herdsmen, wearing their national costume, continue the tradition

Jazz
Jazz is particularly popular in Switzerland, and there are major music festivals in Montreux, Ascona, Solothurn, Aarau and Willisau. Top Swiss musicians include Urs Blöchlinger, Pierre Favre, George Gruntz and Bruno Spörri.

Zürich's Tonhalle

of escorting their herds up to the summer pastures. The open-air performances of the William Tell legend which take place in Interlaken and Altdorf are immensely popular with visitors.

Other cultural attractions for the visitor range from singing competitions, rifle contests and folk dancing to flag-swinging, alphorn-blowing and fights between bulls. The latter, contests for the leadership of the herd, are a speciality of Valais; no blood is shed and the animals are generally very polite to each other. Horse lovers should make a point of visiting the *Marché-Concours*, the horse market in Saignelégier, where an impressive display of chariot racing is among the highlights.

Festival Calendar

January	*Greiflet* in Schwyz, a traditional festival ushering in the *Fasnacht* celebrations; *Schlitteda*, a horse drawn-sled festival, in various parts of the Engadine (including St Moritz).
February	*Fasnacht* festivities, e.g. the *Rabadan* in Bellinzona, the *Fritschi* procession in Luzern and the *Tschägätta-Fasnacht* in the Lötsch Valley.
March	*Chalandamarz* in the Engadine, where village youths drive off evil spirits with large cowbells; *Fasnacht* (carnival celebrations) in Basel with the *Morgenstraich (see page 20).*
April	*Sechseläuten* in Zürich: a large straw doll *(Böögg)* that symbolises winter is burnt to herald spring, and the guilds march in a lengthy procession.
May	*Auffahrts-Umritt* in Beromünster: the evil spirits are driven away yet again, this time by circling one's property.
June	Corpus Christi procession in the Lötsch Valley.

Autumn festivals
Autumn brings the harvest and its related festivals — especially for vine-growers. Cows are brought back down from their summer in the Alps, their heads bedecked with flowers. All through the year, traditional religious festivals are still observed, especially in the Catholic rural areas, where solemn religious processions are a regular feature of country life.

A cowbell at the cattle festival in Umasch

July	Flag-swinging festivals; shepherds' festival on the Gemmi (Kandersteg); Engadine *Konzertwochen* (music festival until mid-August); open-air Paleo rock and folk festival in Nyon; Montreux Jazz Festival.
August	*Fêtes de Genève* – Geneva's city festival including firework display; Alp festival is held in Emmental; *Marché-Concours* horse fair in Saignelégier in the Franches Montagnes.
September	*Chästeilet* cheese festival in Hasliberg, Sigriswil and Schwanden; *Knabenschiessen* in Zürich, shooting competition for young boys; wine festivals are held in Neuchâtel, Locarno and around Lake Thun.
October	*Bénichon de la Montagne* folk festival with cart races in Charmey, Fribourg.
November	Autumn fair in Basel, the oldest and largest in Switzerland; *Zibelemärit* onion festival in Bern.
December	The historical *Escalade* in Geneva; Christmas processions in Beckenried, Fribourg and Bulle; *Chlausjagen* procession (much noise and fancy dress) in Küssnacht on the Rigi.

Below: taking part in the Fasnacht celebrations, Luzern Bottom: a Tschägätta figure in the Lötsch Valley

FOOD AND DRINK

When asked in a survey recently about their favourite spare-time activity, a majority of Zürich's population answered 'eating out'. Switzerland gets a lot of stars of approval for its food abroad, but it is just as popular at home. There's no such thing as a 'national' cuisine, however: Swiss food is a mixture of numerous outside influences, especially French, Italian and Swabian, and there are also a large number of regional delicacies, several of which have found international favour.

Switzerland's culinary favourites emerged from the country's historical patchwork of rather isolated communities whose distinctive diets depended on what was available locally. By the 16th century, people in Ticino were eating rice imported from the Po plain with home-produced pork, goat's milk, chestnuts and wine. In Valais the emphasis was on bread, cheese, dried beef and wine.

The potato only came into its own during a lean period in the 18th century, and it has never looked back, being a feature of many dishes today in the northeast and northwest of the country. In Aargau and Bern, for example, the tradition was born of parboiling, grating and frying the potato, the result known as *rösti*. Ticino shunned the potato but was enthusiastic about corn, which, as polenta, became one of the staples of its diet.

CHEESE

Cheese, of course, is a favourite of Swiss cuisine. One typically Swiss dish is *fondue*, which tastes best when the weather's really cold, and preferably if it's snowing or raining too. That's when you sit down at the hot *caquelon* and use long prongs to dunk portions of bread into hot, melted, *kirschwasser*-flavoured cheese. This filling meal is accompanied by white wine or tea. Another cheese dish that's gaining in popularity is *raclette*, which started out in Valais. In a small tray, sections of cheese are placed over boiled potatoes or other vegetables and then grilled until they go crispy brown.

But cheese doesn't have to be melted to taste good. *Emmentaler* and *Appenzeller* are well known to everyone, and *Gruyère* too. *Vacherin*, only available in the winter, and *Schabziger*, a herbal cheese from Glarus, are both acquired tastes. Specialities from Ticino include *Formaggini* (cheese made from goat's milk) and several mountain cheeses, the most famous of which is probably *Piora*.

But there is more to enjoy than just cheese. One popular speciality is *Zürcher Geschnetzeltes*, veal in a creamy sauce. Another favourite dish, the *Berner Platte*, is even more substantial: a gastronomic selection of pork and sausage served with sauerkraut or beans and boiled potato.

Cakes and chocolate

To round off any meal, or to go with the Swiss version of excellent afternoon coffee known as Z'Vieri, the variety and richness of Swiss cakes and desserts deserve a special mention. You could try Zuger Kirschtorte (cake with kirsch, the popular cherry liqueur), Rüeblitorte (carrot cake) from the Aargau, or Engadiner Nusstorte (layer cake with a nut filling). There is also a variety of meringues with whipped cream and — last but not least — Swiss chocolate, in all its infinite variety. Whether your favourite is creamy milk chocolate or the dark and bitter variety, you will find it here, and know that it is good quality.

Another delicacy from the Bern region is the *rösti (see previous page)*, sometimes with diced bacon.

Soups worth mentioning are *Basler Mehlsuppe* (thick maize soup), *Bündner Gerstensuppe* (barley soup) and – not for the squeamish – *Busecca* (Italian soup made from brains). The most popular dish in Switzerland's sunny south is *polenta*, a paste made from corn which can be prepared with fresh cream or gorgonzola cheese. *Risotto* is also much appreciated beyond the Gotthard, especially when served Milanese style (with saffron) or country style (with vegetables), and the *minestrone* vegetable soup in Ticino is world famous.

In the restaurants on the lakes fish is also very popular, especially trout *(forelle)* and pike *(hecht)* in western Switzerland and perch and fera on Lake Geneva. In late autumn and winter many establishments serve excellent game dishes such as *garnierte Rehrücken* (saddle of venison).

Another very Swiss speciality is *Bündnerfleisch*, air-dried and very thinly-sliced meat. The Valais version of this Grisons speciality is often known as *Walliser Fleisch*.

The grand Hotel Regina in Wengen

WINE

Wine was introduced by the Romans, but it was not until the 9th century that the beer-drinking laity obtained it from the clergy, who used it, of course, for liturgical purposes. By the 19th century production had grown so indiscriminately, and the results become so indifferent, that consumers went back to drinking beer. A wine statute in 1953 imposed rigorous quality controls and since then Swiss wine has improved immensely.

Switzerland produces some excellent wines – white wines in particular. Whether white or red, the wines are light and predominantly dry. The main wine-producing areas are on Lake Geneva and the Lac de Neuchâtel, and also in the Rhône Valley. Famous whites include Dézaley and Saint-Saphorin (Lake Geneva), Fendant and Johannisberg (Valais) and Twanner (Lake Biel). Good reds include Dôle, Pinot Noir (Valais) and Merlot (Ticino).

RESTAURANT SELECTION

The following are suggestions from Switzerland's main centres. We have listed them according to three categories:
€€€ = expensive; €€ = moderate; € = inexpensive.

Basel

Bruderholz-Stucki, Bruderholzallee 42, CH4059 Basle, tel: (061) 361 8222, fax: (061) 361 8203. Probably the best gourmet restaurant in town, with a good-value midday menu. €€€
Gasthof zum Goldenen Stern, St Alban-Rheinweg 70, CH4052 Basel, tel: (061) 272 1666, fax: (061) 272 1667; email: info@sternen-basel.ch; www.sternen-basel.ch Basel's oldest inn with garden restaurant, Rhine terrace; good Swiss fare. €€
Gifthüttli, Schneidergasse 11, CH4051 Basel, tel: (061) 261 1656, fax: (061) 261 1456. Famed for its *röstis* and *Cordon Bleus* dishes. €€

Bellinzona

Locanda Brack, Via delle Vigne, CH6515 Gudo-Progero (13km/7 miles from Bellinzona), tel: (091) 859 1254, fax: (091) 859 2098. Delicious fresh pasta served with seasonal produce, and good wines too. Popular with the locals. €€
Locanda Orico, Via Orico 13, CH6500 Bellinzona, tel: (091) 825 1518, fax: (091) 825 1519; www.locanda orico.ch Very good food, friendly service, large assortment of Ticino cheeses, delicious desserts. €€/€€€

Bern

Frohsinn, Münstergasse 54, CH3000 Bern, tel: (931) 311 3767. Delicious food and not too expensive either. €€
Menuetto, Herrengasse 22, CH3000 Bern, tel: (031) 311 1448. An excellent vegetarian restaurant with absolutely delicious dishes that might tempt even the most carnivorous of customers. €€

Chur

Zum Kornplatz, Kornplatz 1, CH7000 Chur, tel: (081) 252 2759. Popular with young and old, great food with a Grisons touch. €€

Fribourg

Buffet de la Gare CFF, Place de la Gare, CH1700 Fribourg, tel: (026) 322 2816, fax: (026) 323 2745; email: buffet-gare@bluewin.ch; www.buffet-fribourg.ch Unbelievably good food, even though this is in the railway station. €€

Geneva

Parc des Eaux Vives, Quai Gustave Ador 82, CH1211 Geneva, tel: (022) 735 4140, fax: (022) 786 8765. Great food, great wine, superb location, very expensive. €€€
Le Saint-Germain, Boulevard de Saint-Georges 61, CH1201 Geneva, tel/fax: (022) 328 2624. Best seafood in town. €€
Swiss Cottage, Rue Barton 6, CH1200 Geneva, tel: (922) 732 4000. For sheer tourist fun, traditional though unexciting Swiss dishes served with Swiss entertainment – and a good sense of humour. €€
Vieux-Bois, Ecole Hôtelière de Genève, Avenue de la Paix 12, (next to the Pregny entrance to the UN), CH1200 Geneva, tel: (022) 919 2426. Fine cuisine served attentively by aspiring chefs and maître d's. A good place for lunch. €€

Gruyères

Hôtel de Ville, CH1663, Gruyères, tel: (026) 921 2424. This fine establishment on the main street serves a range of local dishes. It has a good terrace for summer dining. €€

Lausanne

Rochat (previously Girardet), Rue d'Yverdon 1, CH1023 Crissier, tel: (021) 634 0505. Even though the famous Swiss chef Fredy Girardet has left, his sous chef Philippe Rochat has maintained the highest quality of food and ambiance and it is still considered Switzerland's best. Reserve way ahead. €€€

Locarno

Centenario, Lungolago Motta 17, CH6600 Locarno, tel: (091) 743 8222. This is the place to come for superb food and service. €€€

Lucerne

Old Swiss House, Löwenplatz 4, CH6000 Lucerne, tel: (041) 410 6171. Excellent ambiance and delicious food and wine, albeit rather expensive. €€€
Wirtshaus Galliker, Schützenstrasse 1, CH6000 Lucerne, tel: (041) 240 1002. Traditional specialities, such as *pot-au-feu* and *leberli* with *rösti*. €

Lugano

Al Portone, Viale Cassarate 3, CH6900 Lugano, tel: (091) 923 5511, fax: (091) 971 6505. Excellent, inventive (and expensive) Italian cuisine in relaxed setting. €€€
Tinera, Via dei Gorini 2, CH6900 Lugano. Very popular, reasonably priced *grotto* specialising in Ticinese and Lombard dishes. €€

Martina

Chasa Engiadina, CH7560 Martina, near customs post, tel: (081) 860 0343, fax: (081) 866 3706. Delicious food served in a house dating from 1645. Self-service option downstairs. €€

Montreux

Auberge de la Cergniaulaz-Orgevaux, CH1833 Les Avants (8km/5 miles from Montreux), tel: (021) 964 4276. Substantial food using only the best ingredients. €€

Naters

Geimerheim, Geimen, CH3904 Naters, tel/fax: (027) 923 7018. Valais specialities and delicious seafood. €

Neuchâtel

Maison des Halles, Rue du Trésor 4, CH2000 Neuchâtel, tel: (032) 724 3141, fax: (032) 721 3084. Very good food served in a 400-year-old building; delicious desserts. €€

Schaffhausen

Zur Gerberstube, Bachstrasse 8, CH8200 Schaffhausen, tel: (052) 625 2155. Excellent Italian food, stylish décor. €€

Solothurn

Zum alten Stephan, Friedhofplatz 10, CH4500 Solothurn, tel: (032) 622 1109, fax: (032) 623 7060; email: email@alterstephan.ch; www.alterstephan.ch Famous restaurant with excellent food in its first floor *Narrenstübli* and street café. €€

Thun

Schloss Schadau, Lake Thun, tel: (033) 222 2500, fax: (033) 222 1580. Superb food served in a castle with a gastronomy museum. €€

Zug

Hecht am See, Fischmarkt 2, CH6300 Zug, tel: (041) 711 0193, fax: (041) 729 8147; email: hecht-zug@datazug.ch; www.hecht.ch Famous for its seafood dishes and excellent wines. €€

Zürich

Bierhalle Kropf, In Gassen 16, CH8001 Zürich, tel: (01) 211 5665. Very filling food, attractive art deco décor. €€
Hiltl Vegi, Sihlstrasse 28, CH8023 Zürich, tel: (01) 227 7000. Just off Bahnhofstrasse, this is the best vegetarian restaurant in town, as well as the oldest – it was founded in 1898. With fifty kinds of salads. €€
Kronenhalle, Rämistrasse 4, CH8001 Zürich, tel: (01) 251 6669. Traditional restaurant, good French cuisine. €€
Zunfthaus zur Saffran, Limmatquai 54, CH8001 Zürich, tel: (01) 251 3740. Local specialities, elegant dining on first floor of old guild house. €€

ACTIVE HOLIDAYS

ALPINE SIGHTSEEING BY PLANE

A bird's eye view of the mountains is available from over 20 different airfields (for details, contact the Switzerland Travel Centre, *see page 119*).

COVERED WAGON TREKS

Covered wagon trekking is a pleasant way to travel. Trips are available through the Emmental and across the Jura. Contact Eurotrek AG, Vulkanstrasse 116, CH8048 Zürich, tel: (01) 434 3366, fax: (01) 434 3344; email: eurotrek@rbm.ch; www.eurotrek.ch

CYCLING AND MOUNTAINBIKING

Cycling has become very popular over the past few years, especially the 'Alpine' variety, as it is an excellent way to see the country. Switzerland is well organised for cyclists, and bicycles (*vélos*) can be hired at all the larger SBB railway stations. For more details visit www.veloland.ch, a site in several languages including English, or contact Switzerland Travel Centre.

GOLF

Switzerland has over 50 golf courses. A brochure is available listing their location and size, obtainable from the Switzerland Travel Centre.

HANG-GLIDING

There are plenty of hang-gliding and paragliding schools and several excellent places to jump off mountains. 'Tandem flights' (with someone else acting as pilot) are also available.

Steamship tours
Several historic steamships do tours of Lake Lucerne, Lake Geneva, Lake Brienz and Lake Zürich. There are also regular ship connections on the Rhine and the Aare.

HIKING AND CLIMBING

With over 50,000km (31,000 miles) of marked hiking routes, there's something for everyone. Those unused to Alpine mountaineering would do better to hire a guide. Ten national hiking routes, covering distances from 200–400km (125–250 miles) traverse the country, with individual stages planned to suit day or weekend hikes.

There are 50 mountaineering schools and regular courses. For information contact local tourist centres.

Leisurely walkers and bikers will find private farm roads are open to them and are a pleasant and relaxed way to enjoy the countryside.

HOT-AIR BALLOONING

Ballooning, though expensive, is popular. For more information contact the Switzerland Travel Centre.

RIVER RAFTING AND HYDROSPEED

River rafting down the Saane, Simme, Upper Rhine, Inn, Lütschine, etc. is exhilarating. Hydrospeed is similar but involves sitting on a small watersled. Contact Eurotrek (*see above*).

WATER SPORTS

Sailing, windsurfing and waterskiing are available on the larger lakes. There are numerous windsurfing, yachting and water-skiing schools.

WINTER SPORTS

Switzerland is a paradise for skiers, with no fewer than 200 winter holiday resorts, 1,870 mountain railways, ski lifts and cable cars, and 5,000km (3,000 miles) of ski runs. The main resorts such as Zermatt, Saas-Fee, St Moritz, Davos, Arosa and Wengen, are world famous for their downhill runs, but for cross-country skiers the Swiss Jura is hard to beat.

PRACTICAL INFORMATION

Getting There

BY AIR

There are regular international connections to the three major airports in Switzerland – Zürich, Basel and Geneva. The new SWISS Air Lines have taken over all the routes previously handled by Swissair and Crossair, with some improvement in service. British Airways and EasyJet also fly regularly from the UK to Switzerland. There are many connection possibilities from the US.

For further information on SWISS, contact: www.swiss.com Or call 0845 601 0956 in the UK, 1800 221 47 50 in the US, 1800 221 339 in Australia, or contact the Switzerland Travel Centre: **In the UK:** Swiss Centre, Swiss Court, London W1V 8EE, Freephone 00800 100 200 30, or Freefax 00800 100 200 31; e-mail: stc@stlondon.com
In the US: Swiss Center, 608 Fifth Avenue, New York, NY; toll free tel: 1800 221 4750. Swiss owned and run, the Switzerland Travel Centre offers comprehensive information and bookings: packages, flights, Eurostar, rail

Air travel was previously more civilised

tickets, passes to and within Switzerland, car hire, motorway vignettes; hotels and holiday apartments.

If proceeding by train, with 'Fly-Rail Baggage' passengers arriving in Switzerland by air via Zürich, Basel or Geneva can check their baggage through to their final destination (all cities and larger resort areas).

BY RAIL

Tickets from London or the Channel ports to the Swiss frontier, or through to principal Swiss destinations, as well as international tickets between major cities, are obtainable from Rail Europe (tel: 0990 848848, European rail travel, motor rail and Eurostar) or its agencies. The quickest way of reaching the continent from the UK is to take the Eurostar service through the Channel Tunnel from London's Waterloo Station (tel: 0990 186186). There are good connections to everywhere in Switzerland on all the main types of European train (ICE, Eurocity, Intercity); do remember, however, to make seat reservations in advance. Travellers should be aware of the special deals and tickets available; ask at your travel agents or at the tourist office *(see page 117)*.

BY CAR

As well as the ferry, visitors from the UK also have the possibility of taking Le Shuttle, the Channel Tunnel service carrying cars and their passengers from Folkestone to Calais on a drive-on-drive-off system. From Calais it is possible to travel by motorway right through to Switzerland. Before entering the country, travellers must pass through the border customs. Don't forget vehicle registration documents, driving licence and country stickers.

Getting Around

BY PLANE

Flights within the country are operated by SWISS Air Lines and Air Engadina. Fly-Rail Baggage *(see above)* allows passengers to check in their plane luggage at railway stations.

BY TRAIN

In Switzerland, Intercity, fast and regional trains have direct connections to all cities and most holiday resort areas. There are approximately 86 trains with dining cars and 325 trains with mini-bars in operation each day. In addition, there are four classic panoramic journeys that can be taken as tours, providing spellbinding views of the country's magnificent scenery: the **William Tell Express** from Lucerne to Lugano, the **Glacier Express** from Zermatt to St Moritz, the **Bernina Express** from Chur to Lugano, the **Golden Pass** from Lucerne to Montreux. Reservations can be made at Swiss railway stations and travel agencies.

Mountain railways

There are around 500 mountain railways that take visitors quickly and comfortably into the mountain world. Included among these are rack-railways, funicular railways, cable cars and chair-lifts, as well as alpine underground railways (for example, the Metro-Alpin in Saas-Fee). Schedules are available in railway stations and at local tourist information centres.

BY POSTBUS

When you get to a place without a railway, hop on one of the yellow buses operated by the Swiss Postal Service. These vehicles not only serve the needs of the remotest areas, but also offer tours throughout the country, such as the famous **Palm Express** from St Moritz to Lugano. During lengthy journeys a generous break is allowed to give travellers plenty of time for a bite to eat.

BY BOAT

Regularly scheduled boats cruise all the Swiss lakes. There are steamships to put you in nostalgic mood on Lac Léman, the Zürichsee, Brienzersee and Lake Luzern. It's also possible to take a trip along the Rhine, Rhône, Aare and Doubs rivers.

SPECIAL DEALS

As the agent for Swiss Federal Railways, Swiss Tourist Information Centres in Europe and overseas provide the latest train schedules as well as the following travel tickets: a **Swiss Card** is valid for one month and allows free travel from the Swiss border to any destination inside the country, plus an unlimited number of train, boat or bus journeys within Switzerland at half price. A **Swiss Pass** provides 16,000km (10,000 miles) of free travel on trains, ships and postbuses and the public transport systems of 35 different towns and cities; private bus companies and cable car operators also do reductions for passholders. The Swiss Pass is valid for four, eight, or 15 days or a whole month. The **Swiss Flexi**

Pass has the same advantages as the Swiss Pass except that it can only be used on a choice of three days within any fortnight.

Children (aged 6–16) travelling without their parents travel for half fare. A **Family Card** can be obtained free of charge which entitles children to travel free if accompanied by at least one parent. There are also **Regional Cards** which offer cheaper travel in restricted areas from spring to autumn (Montreux/Vevey, Waadtland/Valais, Bernese Oberland, Lake Luzern, Grison, Locarno/Ascona, Lugano and Churfirsten/Säntis). For more information on the above offers, contact a Switzerland Tourism office or the Swiss Federal Railways.

BY CAR

Remember that in order to use Swiss motorways you have to buy a *vignette* to stick on the windscreen. These cost SFr40 and are valid from 1 December until 31 January (14 months). They can be purchased at borders, post offices, petrol stations and garages in Switzerland, and in other countries from Switzerland Travel Centre offices.

The maximum speed allowed in built-up areas is 50kmph (30mph), on country roads 80kmph (50mph) and on motorways 120kmph (75mph). Spikes on tyres can only be used between November and March (and never on motorways). Drivers and all passengers over 7 years of age must wear seat belts where fitted. Children under 12 years have to travel in the rear seats. The legal limit for alcohol is 0.8 millilitres, and beware, the Swiss are extremely efficient when it comes to spot-checks.

The following Alpine passes are usually closed from mid-November to mid-May: Albula, San Bernardino (tunnel open all year round), Grosser St Bernhard (tunnel open all year round; toll), Furka, St Gotthard (tunnel open all year round), Grimsel Klausen, Lukmanier, Nufenen, Oberalp, Splügen, Susten and Umbrail.

For more information contact either of the following:
Swiss Touring Club (Touring Club Suisse TCS), Chemin de Blandonnet 4, CH1214 Vernier (Geneva), tel: (022) 417 2350, fax: (022) 417 2382; www.tcs.ch
Swiss Automobile Club (Automobil-Club der Schweiz ACS), Wasserwekgasse 39, CH3000 Bern 13, tel: (031) 311 7722, fax: (031) 311 0310; www.acs.ch

Facts for the Visitor

TRAVEL DOCUMENTS

Travellers from the European Union, the US, Canada, Australia, and New Zealand only need to bring a valid passport, assuming they plan to stay for no longer than three months. Children under 16 not entered in their parents' passports are expected to have child permits (plus a photo) from age 10 onwards.

CUSTOMS REGULATIONS

The following can be brought in duty-free by anyone visiting Switzerland: articles for personal use such as cameras, clothing, sports articles and musical instruments, presents to the value

---

Heritage railways

Switzerland has some of the finest heritage railways in the world, many running steam trains on certain days. Enthusiasts could try the Brienz Rothorn Bahn (Brienz–Rothorn), tel: (033) 952 2222 or the Regionalverkehr (Berne–Solothurn), tel: (031) 925 5555. A further attraction is the Mount Rigi rack railway, also with steam traction.

of SFr300, 2 litres of alcohol, 200 cigarettes or 50 cigars or 250g tobacco.

On leaving the country everyone over 17 is allowed to export the following duty-free: 200 cigarettes or 50 cigars or 250g tobacco, 1 litre of spirits, or presents to a maximum value of SFr300.

There are no limits on the amount of Swiss and foreign currencies that can be taken in or out.

TOURIST INFORMATION

Abroad, information and brochures are available from the following Switzerland Travel Centre offices:
In the UK: Swiss Centre, Swiss Court, London W1V 8EE, tel: 0800 100 200 30; fax 00800 100 200 31; e-mail: stc@stlondon.com
In the US: Swiss Center, 608 Fifth Avenue, New York, NY, tel: 1800 221 4750.

The official website for travel information and reservations is www.My Switzerland.com
Note: if you are accessing from a non-English speaking country and would like access in English, use: http://uk. myswitzerland.com/en/welcome.cfm
Other useful websites are:
www.swissinfo.ch
www.about.ch (for facts about the country rather than travel information)
www.museums.ch (for all the current information on museums and exhibitions in Switzerland).
In Switzerland: contact Switzerland Tourism (Schweiz Tourismus), Tödistrasse 7, CH8027 Zürich, tel: (091) 288 1111, fax: (01) 288 1205.
For more specific regional tourist information, contact:
Aargau, Aargau Tourismus, 4800 Zofingen, tel: (062) 746 2040, fax: (962) 746 2041.
Basel/Basel-Land, Basel Tourismus, Schiffslände 5, CH4001 Basel, tel: (061) 268 6868, fax: (061) 268 6870;

email: office@baseltourismus.ch; www.basel-tourismus.ch
Bernese Jura, Office du Tourisme du Jura Bernois, 26 Av. de la Liberté, CH2740 Moutier, tel: (032) 493 6466, fax: (032) 493 6156; email: information@jurabernois.ch; www.jurabernois.ch
Bernese Oberland, Berner Oberland Tourismus, Jungfraustr. 38, CH3800 Interlaken, tel: (033) 823 0303, fax: (033) 823 0330; e-mail: info@berneroberland.com; www.berneroberland.com, www.berner-oberland-hotels.ch
Central Switzerland, Zentralschweiz Tourismus, CH6002 Luzern, tel: (041) 418 4080, fax: (041) 418 4081; e-mail: info@CentralSwitzerland.ch; www.CentralSwitzerland.ch
Eastern Switzerland and Liechtenstein, Tourismusverband Ostschweiz, Bahnhofsplatz 1a, CH9001 St Gallen, tel: (071) 227 3737, fax: (071) 227 3767; e-mail: info@ostschweiz-i.ch; www.ostschweiz-i.ch
Fribourg, Pays de Fribourg/Freiburgerland Information, CH1644 Avrydevant-Port, tel: (026) 915 9292, fax: (026) 915 9299; e-mail: info.tourisme @pays-de-fribourg.ch; www.pays-de-fribourg.ch
Geneva, Genève Tourisme, Rue du Mont-Blanc 18, CH1201 Geneva 1, tel: (021) 613 2626, fax: (021) 613 2600, Hotels: (022) 909 7020; e-mail: info@geneve-tourisme.ch, hotels: reservation@geneve-tourisme.ch; www.lake-geneva-region.ch
Grisons (Graubünden), Graubünden Holidays, Alexanderstr. 24, CH7001 Chur, tel: (081) 254 2424, fax: (081) 254 2400; e-mail: contact@graubuenden.ch; www.graubuenden.ch
Jura, Jura Tourisme, Siège cantonal, Rue de la Gruère 1, CH2350 Saignelégier, tel: (032) 952 1953, fax: (932) 952 1955; e-mail: administration @juratourisme.ch; www.juratourisme.ch
Lac Léman Region/Vaud, Office du Tourisme du Canton du Vaud, 60 Av. d'Ouchy, Case Postale 164, CH1000 Lausanne 6-Ouchy, tel: (021) 613

2626, fax: (021) 613 2600; e-mail for
Lausanne: information@lausanne-tourisme.ch
Neuchâtel, Neuchâtel Tourismus,
Hôtel des Postes, CH2001 Neuchâtel,
tel: (032) 889 6890, fax: (032) 889
6296; e-mail: tourisme.neuchateloise@ne.ch;
www.ne.ch/tourism
Solothurn, Solothurn Tourismus,
Hauptgasse 69, CH4500 Solothurn,
tel: (032) 626 4646, fax: (032) 626
4647; e-mail: info@solothurn-city.ch; www.
solothurn-city.ch
Swiss Mittelland, Schweizer Mittelland Tourismus c/o Bern Tourismus,
CH3001 Bern, tel: (031) 328 1228,
fax: (031) 311 1222, Hotel-line (031)
328 1210; e-mail: info@smit.ch; www.smit.ch
Ticino, Ticino Turismo, Casella
Postale 1441, CH6501 Bellinzona, tel:
(091) 825 7056, fax: (091) 825 3614;
e-mail: info@tucino-tourismo.ch; www.tucino-
tousimo.ch
Valais, Valais Tourisme/Wallis
Tourismus, Rue Pré-Fleuri 6, CH1951
Sion, tel: (027) 327 3570, fax: (027)
327 3571; e-mail: info@valaistourism.ch;
www.valaistourism.ch, www.matterhornregion.com
Zürich, Zürich Tourismus, Haupt-
bahnhof, CH8023 Zürich, tel: (01) 215
4000, (01) 215 4040 (hotels), fax: (01)
215 4044; e-mail: information@zurich-
tourism.ch, hotel@zurichtourism.ch; www.zurich
tourism.ch

CURRENCY AND EXCHANGE
The unit of currency in Switzerland
is the Swiss franc (SFr), with 100 *rappen* (centimes) to a franc. There are
5, 10 and 20 rappen coins and ½, 1, 2
and 5 franc coins. Notes are issued in
denominations of 10, 20, 50, 100, 500
and 1,000 francs.

Banks, foreign exchange outlets,
travel agencies and the larger hotels
will all exchange foreign currency.
Traveller's cheques in Swiss francs are
accepted at their face value when used
for payments in hotels, restaurants and
shops; those in other foreign currencies are cashed at the current rate of
exchange, less commission. All the
major credit cards are accepted (especially Visa). Money is easily obtained
from bank ATMs.

OPENING TIMES
Banks
Monday to Friday 8.30am–noon and
2–4.30pm.

Government offices
Monday to Friday 8am–noon and
2–6pm.

Post offices
Monday to Friday 7.30am–noon and
1.45–6.30pm, Saturday 7.30–11am
(except for a few major offices in the
cities, which close later).

Shops
Monday to Friday 8am–12.30pm and
1.30–6.30pm, Saturday 8am–12.30pm
and 1.30–4pm; often open at
lunchtime in the cities, and open till
9pm on Wednesday or Thursday.
Most shops in Switzerland are closed
on Monday morning (regional varia-
tions are possible).

Museums
As a general rule, museums are open
at the following times: Tuesday to
Sunday 10am–noon and 2–5pm. Some
larger museums may open in the
evenings on certain days, while
smaller and regional museums are
sometimes only open half-days or at
weekends.

TIPPING
Tips are automatically included on all
hotel and restaurant bills, as well as
at hairdressers and on most taxi fares.
Visitors can leave an extra tip if they
want to, especially in a restaurant if the
service has been outstanding, but it is
not expected.

PUBLIC HOLIDAYS

The following days are public holidays in Switzerland: New Year's Day, Good Friday, Easter Monday, Ascension, Whit Monday, 1 August (National Day) and Christmas Day. Some cantons also celebrate Berchtoldstag (2 January), Corpus Christi (mid-June), Assumption (15 August), All Saints' Day (1 November), Immaculate Conception (8 December) and St Stephen's Day (26 December). Labour Day (1 May) is not universally celebrated.

TELEPHONE

The Swiss phonecard, called Taxcard, allows phone calls to be made from public payphones which are equipped with card readers. PTT Taxcards are on sale for SFr10 and SFr20 at post offices, newsagents, railway stations, etc. To make an international call, dial the international access code (00), then the country code, followed by the area code (omitting any initial 0) and the number. The international country code for Switzerland is 41 (i.e. dial 00 41 from the UK). All local calls now require the area code.

VOLTAGE

The voltage in Switzerland is 220V AC. Suitable adaptors can be bought at electrical goods outlets and most airports; US electrical appliances will need transformers.

CLOTHING

Swiss weather is a mix of continental, Mediterranean, sub-tropical and marine, so be prepared for both warm and cold spells and have an umbrella to hand in case of rain. Sunglasses and sunscreen are necessary all year.

PEOPLE WITH DISABILITIES

General information – especially with regard to suitable accommodation – is available from the Schweizerischer Invalidenverband (SIV), Sektion Schweiz und Umgebung 6430 Schwyz/SZ Postfach 48, CH6431 Schwyz, tel: (041) 811 3661; e-mail: sivinfo@bluewin.ch, and Mobility International, Postfach 129 Feldeggstrasse 77, CH8032 Zürich, tel: (01) 383 0497; www.mis-ch.ch

In addition, the *Schweizerischer Hotelier Verein* (SHV) Hotel Guide designates hotels suitable for disabled visitors with the international wheelchair symbol.

HEALTH AND INSURANCE

As there is no state-funded health service in Switzerland and medical treatment must be paid for, it is strongly recommended that you take out insurance cover against personal accident and sickness.

EMERGENCIES

Police, tel: 117
Fire brigade, tel: 118
Emergency doctor, tel: 144
A 24-hr breakdown service is also available, tel: 140.

DIPLOMATIC REPRESENTATION

UK: Embassy of Great Britain, Thunstrasse 50, 3005 Bern, tel: (031) 359 7700, fax: (031) 359 7701, e-mail: info@britain-in-switzerland.ch; www.britain-in-switzerland.ch Open 8.30am–noon, 1.30–5pm.

British Consulate General, 37–9 rue de Vermont, CH1211 Geneva, tel: (022) 918 2400.

British Vice-Consulate, Hegibachstrasse, CH8032 Zürich, tel: (01) 383 6560, fax: (01) 383 6561.

US: US Embassy, American Citizens Services, Jubilaeumstrasse 93, 3005 Bern, tel: (031) 357 7234 or (031) 357 7011, fax: (031) 357 7344, www.usembassy.ch Open 8.30am–12.30 and 1.30–5.30pm.

ACCOMMODATION

HOTELS

The standard of accommodation in Switzerland is generally high. Hotels that are members of the Swiss Hotel Association (*Schweizerischer Hotelier Verein* – SHV) are divided into five categories with between one and five stars. Accommodation usually includes breakfast, service charge and taxes. Out of peak season, many places offer inexpensive all-inclusive deals. The SHV publishes a guide to 3,500 hotels and pensions in book or CD-ROM form, available from the Switzerland Travel Centre *(see page 119)*.

The Travel Centre can also help make reservations. Advance reservations at peak times are advisable; in holiday resorts this is generally from July to early September, over Christmas and New Year and February to mid-March. Towns are busy during trade fairs and other important events.

YOUTH HOSTELS

The Swiss Youth Hostel Association (SJH) has over 80 different establishments across the country, open to people of all ages, as long as they can show a valid membership card. Families and leaders of larger travel groups need special permits. These can be obtained from the SJH in Zürich, who also provide a directory that lists all the hostels. Swiss Youth Hostels Association, Schaffhauserstrasse 14, CH8042 Zürich, tel: (01) 360 1414, fax: (01) 360 1460; e-mail: bookingoffice@youthhostel.ch; www. youthhostel.ch

FARMHOUSE HOLIDAYS/ HOLIDAY APARTMENTS

For farmhouse holidays contact the Switzerland Travel Centre, local tourist offices, or www.bauernhof-ferien.ch or Schweizer Reisekasse (Reka), Neuengasse 15, CH 3001 Bern, tel: (031) 329 6633, fax: (031) 329 6601; www.reka.ch And www.homestay.ch offers information on B&Bs. A catalogue is offered by Rolf Suter, Bernstrasse 6, CH 3067 Boll, tel/fax: (031) 839 7484.

For holiday apartments, local tourist offices *(see page 119)* will have complete and up to date information.

HOTELS

The following are listed according to three categories: €€€ = expensive; €€ = moderate; € = inexpensive.

Basel

Kunsthotel Teufelhof, Leonhardsgraében 47, CH4051, tel: (061) 261 1010, fax: (061) 261 1004; e-mail: info@teufelhof.com; www.teufelhof.com Eight rooms in which artists are given free rein to create a 'gallery', a great restaurant and a theatre. €€€

Merian am Rhein, Rheingasse 2, CH4005, tel: (061) 685 1111, fax: (061) 685 1101; e-mail: kontakt@ merian-hotel.ch; www.merian-hotel.ch Great view of river. Top fish restaurant. €€€

Resslirytti, Theodorsgraben 42, CH4058, tel: (061) 691 6641, fax: (061) 691 4590; e-mail: resslirytti @datacomm.ch. Modern hotel near Mustermesse. €€

Bergün

Hotel Sonnenheim, CH7482, tel: (081) 407 1129, fax: (081) 407 2388; e-mail: hotel.sonnenheim@schweiz.org; www. sonnenheim.ch The restaurant serves excellent Grisons specialities. €

Bern

Hotel Belle Epoque, Gerechtigkeitstrasse 18, CH3011, tel: (031) 311 4336, fax: (031) 311 3936; e-mail: info@belle-epoque.ch; www.belle-epoque.ch Seventeen rooms in a central location, furnished with beautiful antiques. €€€

Bellevue Palace, Kochergasse 3–5, CH3001, tel: (031) 320 4545, fax: (031) 311 4743; e-mail: direction@ bellevue-palace.ch; www.bellevue-palace.ch View of the Alps and top cuisine. €€€

Goldener Schlüssel, Rathausgasse 72, CH3011, tel: (031) 311 0216, fax: (031) 311 5688; e-mail: info@goldener-schluessel.ch; www.goldener-schluessel.ch. Old town architecture and atmospheric restaurant near the city centre. €€

Biel/Bienne

Elite, Bahnhofstrasse 14, CH2501, tel: (032) 328 7777, fax: (032) 328 7770; e-mail: mail@hotelelite.ch; www.hotelelite.ch Traditional hotel in town centre; with a bar and a very good restaurant. €€€

Kreuz, Hauptstrasse 15, CH2514 Ligerz (13km/7 miles from Biel), tel: (032) 315 1115, fax: (032) 315 2814; e-mail: kreuz-ligerz@bluewin.ch; www.kreuz-ligerz.ch Rural inn on the northern shore of Lake Biel, with sauna and family-owned vineyard. €€€

Brienz am See

Hostellerie Lindenhof, CH3855, tel: (033) 952 2030, fax: (033) 952 2040; e-mail: info@hotel-lindenhof.ch; www.hotel-lindenhof.ch. Chalet style with spectacular views. Ideal for families. €€

Burgdorf

Emmenhof, Kirchbergstr, 70, CH3400, tel: (034) 422 2275, fax: (034) 423 4629. Attractive hotel in a converted farmhouse. €€

Stadthaus, Kirchbühl 2, CH3402, tel: (034) 428 8000, fax: (034) 428 8008; e-mail: info@ stadthaus.ch; www.stadthaus.ch Built in 1745 as the town hall, the Stadthaus is now a luxurious hotel with 18 rooms, an elegant restaurant, vaulted wine cellar and fumoir. €€€

Chur

Duc de Rohan, Masanserstrasse 44, CH7000, tel: (081) 252 1022, fax: (081) 252 4537; e-mail: info@ducderohan. ch; www.ducderohan.ch Luxury hotel with fitness club and indoor pool. €€€

Stern, Reichsgasse 11, CH7000, tel: (081) 252 3555, fax: (081) 252 1915; e-mail: stern@romantikhotel.ch; www.stern-chur.ch Historic hotel, edge of old town. Cosy restaurant; local dishes. €€

Einsiedeln

Linde, Schmiedenstrasse 28, CH8840, tel: (055) 418 4848, fax: (055) 418 4849; e-mail: hotel@linde-einsiedeln.ch; www.linde-einsiedeln.ch Close to the abbey; good rooms; excellent restaurant. €€

Ernen

Alpenblick, CH3995, tel: (027) 971 1537, fax: (027) 971 4374; e-mail: info@alpenblickernen.ch; www.alpenblickernen.ch Chalet-style hotel with beautiful views across the alps. Good restaurant. €

Fribourg

De La Rose, Rue de Morat 1, CH1700, tel: (026) 351 0101, fax: (026) 351 0100; e-mail: info@hotel delarose.ch; www.hotelrose.ch Centrally located hotel with good service. €€

Duc Berthold, Rue des Bouchers 5, CH1700, tel: (026) 350 8100, fax: (026) 350 8181; e-mail: ducberthold fribourg@bluewin.ch Next to the cathedral; swimming pool; very good food. €€€

Fuldera

Staila, CH7533, tel: (081) 858 5160, fax: (081) 858 5021; e-mail: info@ hotelstaila.ch Quiet family hotel in the upper Val Müstair; vegetarian specialities. €€

Geneva

Domaine de Châteauvieux, Peney-Desous, CH1412 Satigny, tel: (022) 753 1511, fax: (022) 753 1924; e-mail: chateauvieux@romantikhotels.com; www.romantik hotels.com/Satigny First-class castle hotel set among vineyards. €€€

Hotel de la Paix, Quai de Mont Blanc 911, CH1211, tel: (022) 909 6000, fax: (022) 909 6001; e-mail: reservation@hoteldelapaix.ch; www.hoteldelapaix.ch Large luxury hotel in old traditional-style building along the lakeside. €€€

Luserna, Avenue Luserna 12, CH1203, tel: (022) 949 5656, fax: (022) 949 5636; e-mail: hotel.luserna@span.ch; www.geneva.yop.ch/hotels/luserna Quiet hotel with large garden on the edge of the city, close to the UN. €€

Lausanne

Lausanne-Palace & Spa, Grand-Chêne 7-9, CH1002, tel: (021) 331 3131, fax: (021) 323 2571; e-mail: reservation@lausanne-palace.ch; www.lausanne-palace.ch Luxurious Edwardian landmark; superb view of Lake Geneva and the Alps; one bar designed by Swiss artist Jean Tinguely. €€€

Jeunotel, Chemin du Bois-de-Vaux 36, CH1007, tel: (021) 626 0222, fax: (021) 626 0226; e-mail: jeunotel@urbanet.ch; www.jeunotel.ch Modern, somewhat spartan hotel in lush green surroundings near Lausanne; Sud autoroute exit. €

Locarno

Centovalli, CH6652 Ponte Brolla, tel: (091) 796 1444, fax: (091) 796 3159; e-mail: centovalli@freesurf.ch An inn 4km (2½ miles) from Locarno towards Valle Maggia. Fine cuisine. €

Mirafiori, Via al Parco 25, CH6644 Locarno-Orselina, tel: (091) 743 1877, fax: (091) 743 7739; e-mail: info@mirafiori.ch; www.mirafiori.ch Pleasant hotel overlooking Locarno; pool, garden, playroom. Free bikes. €€

Ramada-Treff Hotel Arcadia, Lungolago G. Motta, CH6600, tel: (091) 756 1818, fax (091) 756 1828; e-mail: arcadia@ramada-treff.ch; www.ramada-treff.ch Large apartments with balconies overlooking lake; pool, sauna, free child care, playroom. €€€

Lucerne

Hotel Chateau Gütsch, Kanonenstrasse, CH6003, tel: (041) 249 4100, fax: (041) 249 4191; e-mail: info@chateau-guetsch.ch; www.château-guetsch.ch First-class hilltop castle hotel; view over Lucerne and the lake. Access by car or private funicular. €€€

Hotel-Restaurant zum Rebstock, St Leodegar Strasse 3, CH6006, tel: (041) 410 3581, fax: (041) 410 3917; e-mail: rebstock@hereweare.ch; www.hereweare.ch Centrally located half-timbered houses; every room uniquely decorated. Friendly, good value restaurant. €€

Sonnegg, Hauptstrasse 37, CH6045 Meggen, tel: (041) 377 4400, fax: (041) 377 4940; e-mail: hotel@sonnegg-meggen.ch; www.sonnegg-meggen.ch Train and bus connections to Lucerne; excellent base for excursions. €

Wilden Mann, Bahnhofstrasse 30, CH6000, tel: (041) 210 1666, fax: (041) 210 1629; e-mail: mail@wilden-mann.ch; www.wilden-mann.ch Small and attractive hotel dating back to 1517, in the old town. Two good restaurants. €€€

Lugano

Ticino, Piazza Cioccaro 1, CH6901, tel: (091) 922 7772, fax: (091) 923 6278; e-mail: romantikhotelticino@ticino.com; www.romantikhotels.com/Lugano Small but excellent hotel in the heart of the old town, near the lake. Completely renovated, with a well known gourmet restaurant. €€

Camping
Of Switzerland's total of 900 campsites, 90 are open all year round. They all appear on an annually updated list available from the Swiss Camping Association (VSC), Seestrasse 119, CH3800 Interlaken, tel: (033) 823 3523, fax: (033) 923 2991; www.camping.ch Information is also available from the Switzerland Travel Centre.

Villa Principe Leopoldo, Via Montalbano 5, CH6900, tel: (091) 985 8855, fax: (091) 985 8825; e-mail: info@leopoldohotel.com; www.leopoldohotel.com Former residence of Prince Leopold of Hohenzollern, magnificently situated above the Collina d'Oro. €€€

Maloja
Hotel Bellavista, CH7516, tel: (081) 824 3195, fax: (081) 824 3208. Good hotel with delicious Mediterranean food. €€

Montreux
Le Montreux Palace, Grand-Rue 100, CH1820, tel: (021) 962 1212, fax: (021) 962 1717; e-mail: sales@montreux-palace.com; www.montreux-palace.com An outstanding Belle Epoque hotel on the shores of Lake Geneva. €€€
Villa Toscane, Rue du Lac 2–8, CH1820, tel: (021) 963 8421, fax: (021) 963 8426; e-mail: villatoscane@montreux.ch; www.montreux.ch/villa-toscane Art nouveau villa overlooking lake promenade; garden terrace, sauna/solarium; opposite Stravinski Auditorium and Congress Centre. €€

Neuchâtel
La Maison du Prussien, Au Gor de Vauseyon, CH2006, tel: (032) 730 5454, fax: (032) 730 2143; e-mail: info@hotel-prussien.ch; www.hotel-prussien.ch This luxurious hotel was a brewery in the 18th century; with a fine restaurant. €€
Du Vaisseau, CH2016 Cortaillod (9km/5 miles southwest of Neuchâtel), tel: (032) 843 4477, fax: (032) 843 4475; e-mail: admin@hotel-le-vaisseau.ch Family hotel between lake and vineyards; beach; excellent cuisine. €€

Pontresina
Walther, CH7504, tel: (081) 839 3636, fax: (081) 839 3637; e-mail: info@hotelwalther.ch; www.hotelwalther.ch Belle

Epoque hotel with pool, fitness centre and tennis court. €€€

Poschiavo
Suisse, Livio Tuena-Triacca, CH7742, tel: (081) 844 0788, fax: (081) 844 1967; e-mail: hotel@suisse-poschiavo.ch; www.suisse-poschiavo.ch Pleasant hotel in centre. €€

S-Charl
Gasthaus Mayor, CH7550, tel: (081) 864 1412, fax: (081) 864 9983. Delightful inn with friendly service on the edge of Swiss National Park. €

Schaffhausen
Rheinhotel Fischerzunft, Rheinquai 8, CH8200, tel: (052) 632 0505, fax: (052) 632 0513; e-mail: info@fischerzunft.ch; www.fischerzunft.ch Comfortable hotel right on the Rhine. €€€

Silvaplana
Hotel Julier Palace, CH7513, tel: (081) 828 9644, fax: (081) 834 3003, e-mail: hotel@julierpalace.com; www.julier palace.com Family place; good food. €€
Sonne, Via Maistra, CH7513, tel: (081) 828 8152, fax: (081) 828 8021. Comfortable and central. €€

Sion
Du Rhône, Rue du Scex 10, CH1951, tel: (027) 322 8291, fax: (027) 323 1188; e-mail: durhonesion@bestwestern.ch; www.bestwestern.ch Pleasant hotel in central location. €€

Solothurn
Baseltor, Hauptgasse 49, CH4500, tel: (032) 622 3422, fax: (032) 622 1879; e-mail: post@baseltor.ch; www.baseltor.ch Centrally located; good menu. €€
Krone, Hauptgasse 64, CH4500, tel: (032) 626 4444, fax: (032) 626 4445; e-mail: reservation@ hotelkrone-solothurn.ch; www.hotelkrone-solothurn.ch Traditional hotel in the Old Town. €€€

St Gallen

Krone, CH9043 Trogen, at end of St Gallen-Speicher-Trogen tramway, tel: (071) 343 6080, fax: (071) 344 4376. Magnificent 18th-century Appenzeller house with façade frescoes. Excellent cooking. **€**

St Moritz

Chesa Guardalej, CH7512 St Moritz-Champfer (4km/2 miles outside of town), tel: (081) 836 6300, fax: (081) 836 6301; e-mail: info@chesa-guardalej.ch; www.chesa-guardalej.ch Quiet, pretty hotel with very good restaurant. **€€€**
Soldanella, CH7500, tel: (081) 833 3651, fax: (081) 833 2337; e-mail: info@hotel-soldanella.ch; www.hotel-soldanella.ch Nicely situated on mountain slope. **€€**

Tarasp

Schlosshotel Chastè, CH7553, tel: (081) 861 3060, fax: (081) 861 3061; e-mail: chaste@bluewin.ch; www.relaischateaux.ch Modern and comfortable, excellent Grisons food. **€€€**

Wengen

Edelweiss, CH3823, tel: (033) 855 2388, fax: (033) 855 4288; e-mail: edelweiss@vch.ch; www.vch.ch/edelweiss Family hotel near the station; sauna. **€€**
Hotel Regina, CH3823, tel: (033) 856 5858, fax: (033) 856 5850; e-mail: regina@wengen.com; www.wengen.com/hotel/regina Grand, century-old hotel overlooking village. **€€€**

Winterthur

Krone, Marktgasse 49, CH8400, tel: (052) 208 1818, fax: (052) 208 1820; e-mail: info@kronewinterthur.ch; www.kronewinterthur.ch Historical, recently renovated hotel in the heart of the Old Town. **€€**
Zum Engel, Wesenplatz 6, CH8416 Flaach, tel: (052) 318 1303, fax: (052) 318 1974. Situated 12km (7 miles) northwest of Winterthur in hiking and water-sports region. **€**

Zermatt

Hotel Dufour, Riedstrasse 35, CH3920, tel: (027) 966 2400, fax: (027) 966 2401. This small, central hotel is a picture postcard Swiss chalet.
Julen, Steinmatte, CH3920, tel: (027) 966 7600, fax: (027) 966 7676; e-mail: hotel.julen@zermatt.ch; www.zermatt.ch/julen Beautifully appointed chalet-style rooms with pool, sauna, steam room, fitness centre. Centrally located. **€€€**

Zug

City-Hotel Ochsen, Kolinplatz 11, CH6300, tel: (041) 729 3232, fax: (041) 729 3222; e-mail: info@ochsen-zug.ch; www.ochsen-zug.ch Traditional hotel in the middle of town. **€€€**

Zuoz

Crusch Alva, CH7524, tel: (081) 854 1319, fax: (081) 854 2459; e-mail: hotel-cruschalva@bluewin.ch; www.cruschalva-zuoz.ch Stylish Engadine hotel with restaurant. **€€€**

Zürich

Glockenhof, Sihlstrasse 31, CH8023, tel: (01) 225 9191, fax: (01) 225 9292; e-mail: info@glockenhof.ch; www.glockenhof.ch Traditional, first-class hotel near the station, with garden restaurant. **€€€**
Landgasthof Leuen, Birmensdorferstrasse 56, CH8142 Uitikon Waldegg, tel: (01) 406 1500, fax: (01) 406 1515; e-mail: info@leuen.ch; www.leuen.ch High above Zürich, this is an ideal base for exploring the surrounding region. Excellent food. **€€**
Scheuble, Mühlegasse 17, CH8001, tel: (01) 268 4800, fax: (01) 268 4801; e-mail: info@scheuble.ch; www.scheuble.ch Stylish rooms in the heart of the Old Town. **€€**
Zürcherhof, Zähringerstrasse 21, CH8025, tel: (01) 269 4444, fax: (01) 269 4445; e-mail: zuercherhof@active.ch; www.bestwestern.ch/zuercherhof Popular with business people. Famous restaurant. **€€**

INDEX